Praise for *Overcoming Conflict*

Unless you are living a life of total solitude, it is inevitable that you are going to face conflict with other people. For the last 14 years I have been able to witness how Bob has handled conflict within a large organization, and I can tell you there is no one more qualified to give us some much needed wisdom on this topic. This book will equip you to not only understand and deal with conflict much more efficiently and successfully but also save you an incredible amount of dumb tax that most people end up paying themselves.

Chris Brown, senior pastor, North Coast Church,
with ministry in four campus locations.

Through the years, Bob Phillips' writings on relationships have been a "go to" source when helping individuals and couples navigate the nuances within of the human condition. Once again Bob has placed at our fingertips a tool which allows the reader to gain insight into the causes of conflict, while offering practical applications toward its resolution.

David P. Ferreira, Ph.D.—a licensed Marriage,
Family, Child Therapist in private practice.

An easy read that cuts deep into one's soul. In these lucid words I found a wealth of wisdom for everyday peacekeeping. The simplicity of the writing is just a disguise for the deep undercurrent of self-assessment and discovery. I found the contents indispensable fuel for personal growth towards relational maturity. This is a workbook for the serious peacemaker.

Quintus Smit, African continent director
for the Pointman Leadership Institute.

Dr. Phillips has used his academic knowledge, together with his vast practical experience, to produce an invaluable "toolkit" for dealing with the ever increasing problem of relationship conflict. It is written in plain words, is very well researched, and can be easily understood by people of all backgrounds and persuasions. Above all, this work shows the author's concern for people. For me, this makes it stand alone.

David Kendrick OBE, QPM—Commander (ret.)
Metropolitan Police Service, London, U.K.

You are about to read the best written and most helpful book I have read in years. I have known Dr. Bob Phillips for more than four decades and can testify that as a biblical psychologist he has spent a lifetime counseling, teaching, and working with thousands of people. He addresses two difficult subjects—anger management and how to confront it. You will find He has poured out his heart, which is saturated in God's Word, and his practical experiences of helping thousands find remedies so you can help others.

> **Tim LaHaye,** D.Min, Litt.D.—author and minister. He wrote more than 40 books, and his Left Behind series is the best-selling Christian fiction series of all time.

I found this book to be an insightful account of every aspect of conflict including its sources, the impact of social styles, and strategies for tackling it. It's a *must-read* for everyone. It's a helpful guide for dealing with relational conflict at home, at work, and in social settings. I wish I had read it at the beginning of my career. It's truly a relationship-handling masterclass.

> **Michael Askew, MSc**—an associate with the UK College of Policing.

In the field of politics, leaders face many difficult problems and issues. A large number of these concerns involve people who are in disagreement with each other. *Overcoming Conflict* is a great resource for anyone who deals with the public. Dr. Bob Phillips is an extraordinary communicator who is able to connect with audiences in different cultures, languages, and backgrounds. I have personally seen him handling difficult situations as a mediator.

> **Napoleon Ardaya, MA**—journalist, author, speaker and consultant on leadership, communication, and politics. He is a former member of the National Congress of the Republic of Bolivia.

The essence of effective diagnosis is asking the right questions before attempting a healing solution. The nature of effective shepherding is deeply caring about the people to whom we are attempting to give those healing answers. Here in his book, *Overcoming Conflict*, Bob Phillips, does both. As a master observer and a skilled helper, Bob presents a wide range of practical tools that provoke our deeper understanding of conflict and stimulate us to loving and restorative action. Professionals and laymen alike will find this a long-lasting and valuable resource.

James M. Cecy, senior pastor-teacher, Campus Bible Church of Fresno,
author and international speaker, and president,
JARON Ministries International, Inc.

As a CEO with close to 700 employees, I have had my share of dealing with personnel conflict within the ranks of my company over the years. Conflict and squabbles are certain to occur, and they will cripple an organization if not dealt with in a healthy and effective manner. With step-by-step instruction, Phillips takes a fresh and comprehensive approach to this age-old problem with tremendous insights in identifying, confronting, and resolving these issues to positive resolution. From start to finish, this book has proven to be an effective tool in my arsenal that I keep within reach on my desk.

Ron Strand, president/CEO, Calico Building Services, Inc.

In clear, understandable words, without techno-babble, Dr. Phillips walks alongside, guiding us in a useful, logical progression to transition from the unproductive, defeating cycle of conflict to positive and successful relationships, dispelling myths and misconceptions along the way. Interlaced with real-life case studies, useful charts, word lists, and checklists, this well-written book lives up to its title and is a must-read, life-changing guidebook for everyone.

Bob Chadwick, D.Jur., LL.M., Brigadier General,
U.S. Marine Corps (ret.)

Dr. Phillips provides valuable insights into how to deal with conflict resolution. Some key examples illustrated in his book include: conducting your conversation in a neutral place, observing the person's body language, and practicing active listening to reduce conflict. There are excellent illustrations found in his book with applicability in the day-to-day circumstances we encounter. With 33 years of client executive experience with IBM, I highly recommend and endorse this book.

Mark Zasso, client executive, IBM Corporation, winner of the
2012 Louis V. Gerstner Award for Client Excellence.

Bob Phillips got my attention with this poke-in-the-ribs: *"It has been suggested that by the time we're in our mid-sixties that we've spent several thousand hours in some form of conflict."* Oh, my. In any other area of life and work requiring thousands of hours, we would study diligently to master the subject. So when is the last time you read a book on relational conflict? Never, probably. Now's the time—and this is the book. It's powerful! I should have read this book 25 years ago!

John Pearson, nationally known board governance and management consultant, John Pearson Associates, Inc. and author of *Mastering the Management Buckets.*

A book you buy should fulfill a need, help you become more effective, and be enjoyable to read. This book reaches all three of these purposes. It provides a plethora of insight on this common challenge we all face, helps the reader understand the many forces in play and most importantly gives the insights to prepare and execute successful resolutions. I have worked with the author as a consultant in several situations where we employed these principles. They work.

Robert L. Vernon, author of *L.A. Justice,* and president of the Pointman Leadership Institute.

OVERCOMING CONFLICT

BOB PHILLIPS

HARVEST HOUSE PUBLISHERS
EUGENE, OREGON

Editing by Barbara Gordon, Eugene, OR
Cover by Bryce Williamson, Eugene, OR
Cover Images © alphaspirit / Shutterstock; posteriori / iStock

This book contains stories in which the author has changed people's names and some details of their situations in order to protect their privacy.

OVERCOMING CONFLICT

Copyright © 2017 Bob Phillips
Published by Harvest House Publishers
Eugene, Oregon 97408
www.harvesthousepublishers.com

ISBN 978-0-7369-6810-2 (pbk.)
ISBN 978-0-7369-6811-9 (eBook)

Library of Congress Cataloging-in-Publication Data
Names: Phillips, Bob, 1940- author.
Title: Overcoming conflict / Bob Phillips.
Description: Eugene, Oregon : Harvest House Publishers, [2017] | Includes
    bibliographical references.
Identifiers: LCCN 2016030267 (print) | LCCN 2016035970 (ebook) | ISBN
    9780736968102 (pbk.) | ISBN 9780736968119
Subjects: LCSH: Conflict management—Religious aspects—Christianity. |
    Interpersonal conflict—Religious aspects—Christianity.
Classification: LCC BV4597.53.C58 P63 2017 (print) | LCC BV4597.53.C58
    (ebook) | DDC 248.8/86—dc23
LC record available at https://lccn.loc.gov/2016030267

Printed in the United States of America

19 20 21 22 23 24 25 / BP-SK / 10 9 8 7 6 5 4

Acknowledgments

In the process of preparing for a seminar on conflict resolution I researched quite a few books dealing with conflict. One of the books was titled *Resolving Conflict at Work*. This was my first introduction to Kenneth Cloke.

I was impressed by many of Dr. Cloke's thoughts on the subject of conflict. As a result, I signed up and attended his mediation training at the Center for Conflict Resolution in Santa Monica, California.

After preparing for and delivering an all-day seminar on conflict resolution I decided to write on the subject. When the manuscript was completed, I reviewed it and thought about various comments Dr. Cloke had shared in his writings and in his classes.

I then approached Dr. Cloke and asked for his permission to include them in this book. I also asked if he would be open to writing a foreword, which he most graciously granted.

Kenneth Cloke is a mediator, arbitrator, attorney, coach, consultant, and trainer. He has taught at the Southwestern University School of Law, Antioch University, Occidental College, USC, and UCLA. He has been involved in mediation work in 24 countries and is the president and cofounder of Mediators Beyond Borders. He has been an arbitrator and mediator for more than 28 years in labor management disputes and is a member of a number of arbitration panels.

I want to publically thank him for writing the foreword and letting me use his quotations, and for his service to mankind.

Bob Phillips

Contents

The Crossroads of Conflict

Every conflict we experience, no matter how trivial, points us toward a crossroads in our lives. One path leads us into anger, fear, confrontation, and bitterness and draws us into quarrels over the past. This path reveals a deep level of caring about outcomes, yet it also encourages adversarial relationships, sterile communications, contemptuous ideas, negative emotions, and unpleasant physical sensations, blinding us and dissipating our energy and spirit. This is the path of impasse, aggression, and antagonism.

A second path leads us into empathy, acceptance, honesty, and mutual respect and draws us into negotiations over the future. This path reveals a deep level of caring about people, and encourages supportive relationships, improved communications, creative ideas, positive emotions, and pleasant physical sensations, making us more conscious and releasing our energy and spirit from destructive conflicts. This is the path of resolution, collaboration, and mutual problem solving.

In addition to these is a third path branching off from the second and largely hidden from view. This path leads us into increased awareness, compassion, integrity, and heartfelt communications and draws us into awareness of the present. It integrates the honesty and caring about outcomes encountered on the first path with the empathy and caring about people encountered on the second. It encourages openhearted relationships, deep learning, intimate communications, profound ideas, poignant emotions, and physical renewal. It wakes us up, makes us more mindful of ourselves and others, and nurtures our energy and spirit. This is the path of transformation and transcendence, of wisdom, spirit, and heart.

In this way, every conflict leads us to two different crossroads. In the beginning, we face a choice between fighting and problem solving. Later, we face a subtler, more arduous and far-reaching choice between merely settling our conflicts and seeking to learn from them, correcting our behaviors, and moving toward forgiveness and reconciliation.

Initially, conflicts entrap us, tempting us along the first path with rewards that cater to our short-term self-interests with personal advantages, fantasies of victory, righteous anger, vengeful pleasures, and the malignant, self-aggrandizing energy of hatred. Yet by accepting these rewards we place our lives on hold, stroke our anger, and magnify our fear of defeat, shame, and loss of self. At the same time, we gratify our opponents and solidify the very thing we resist or object to, creating knots, insensitivities, and places of blindness inside us. These not only make our pains and sacrifices meaningless, they discourage us from following the more difficult, yet ultimately more rewarding path of negotiation, dialogue, and resolution, and the still more difficult and rewarding path of the heart, leading to transformation and transcendence.

Why do so many of us prefer the first path? Partly because we allow our capacity for respectful communication, openheartedness, and integrity to become *conditional* and dependent on the reciprocal actions of others. Partly because we reserve the full exercise of our empathy and honesty for pleasant experiences and supportive relationships. Partly because we are encouraged by media and culture to accept adversarial approaches to conflict that are physically injurious, intellectually one-sided, emotionally unbalanced, spiritually self-defeating, and socially divisive. Partly because others reward us for adversarial behaviors with attention, sympathy, special privileges, a strong sense of identity, distractions from self-hatred, excuses for failure, and reasons for preserving relationships that might otherwise fall apart.

More deeply, no one gets into conflicts over issues that don't matter to them, even if they seem trivial to others. Every conflict therefore involves an element of caring—perhaps concerning content, process, relationship, or how we are being perceived or treated. Mediators and conflict resolution professionals have largely ignored this element of caring, failing to explore the nature and how it might be possible turn distorted, negative communications into connections that are direct, positive, and heartfelt.

Adversarial approaches to conflict stress our bodies, close our minds, and magnify our negative emotions. They weaken our spirits, silence our hearts and undermine our capacity for honest, empathetic communications and intimacy in relationships. They confuse us with false options and dead-end approaches. Worse, they divide us— not only from each other, but from internal parts of ourselves. They cause us to lose perspective and reject whatever our opponents propose. In response, we act defensively, grow intransigent, and ignore or deny whatever we contributed to making the conflict worse. As a result, adversarial conflicts weaken our will, make us unhappy, and cause us to learn little or nothing—other than how right we were.

By following the first path we discover that the advantages it promises are ultimately false, cloying, superficial, and dissatisfying. By resisting its pull and discovering its hidden dynamics, we reveal the presence of the second path, consisting of constructive engagement with our opponents and a mutual search for resolution. This path allows us to transform conflicts from adversarial contests in which everyone loses into dialogues and collaborative negotiations in which everyone can win or at least bear their defeats equally.

By following the second path we discover the third path and recognize that our true opponent and adversary in every conflict is always ourselves, and that the real purpose of the conflict is, has always been, and can only be to reveal what stands in the way of our learning and growth, our development of character, and our capacity for empathy and honesty, integrity and intimacy, caring and compassion.

In the process, we realize that the very conflicts that get us stuck in pointless, seemingly superficial, adversarial battles are the source of outcomes so weighty and profound, so poignant and beautiful that they are impossible to describe in words, yet nearly everyone has experienced them. We are able to discover, in the thick of discord, how to free ourselves from its all-consuming grip, and how to gain insight into what got us stuck. This insight enables us to transform the ways we interact with our opponents by experiencing criticisms and complaints as suggestions for improvement, allowing us to evolve to higher levels of conflict and resolution.

Every conflict presents countless opportunities, both to mediators and parties in conflict, to improve their dispute resolution skills, along with their capacity for wisdom, openheartedness, clarity, balance, and inner peace under trying adversarial conditions. Every conflict therefore leads simultaneously to impasse, to resolution, and to learning, growth, and transcendence.

How, you may ask in the paroxysm of conflict, can you find your way to these second and third paths? The answer is to:

- Move skillfully and steadily into the *heart* of conflict and do battle first and foremost with your desire to travel the seemingly easier, more seductive path of demonization, victimization, powerlessness, and self-righteousness.

- Resist the temptation to compromise or simply settle disputes, or even resolve the underlying issues that gave rise to them.

- Be so deeply committed to yourself and your opponent that you are willing to initiate open, honest, vulnerable conversations and work *through* your conflict, rather than around it.

- Consider your opponent not as an enemy combatant, but as a teacher, partner, citizen, and collaborator.

- Refuse to accept what is inauthentic or heartless, either in your opponent or in yourself.

- Move heroically into the heart of your conflict, where resolution, transformation, and transcendence suddenly, inexplicably, exquisitely unfold.

Transformation and transcendence are therefore present as *possibilities* at every moment, in every conflict. To locate these possibilities, we need to assume that even the most senseless conflicts have the power to significantly alter and improve our lives and, at the simplest level, they do.

As mediators we can help people turn even trivial conflicts into exercises that improve their skills by:

- asking people to pay careful attention to what is done, said, and felt in conflict
- pointing them toward the origin of the conflict inside them and their opponents
- encouraging them to listen with open hearts and minds
- inviting them to jointly search for solutions that satisfy everyone's underlying interests
- strengthening their personal and social capacity for empathy, honesty, and integrity
- making it possible for each person to forgive themselves and others without condoning the harm they or their opponents have caused
- enabling them to repair and redesign the dysfunctional systems that chronically generated the conflict
- assisting others in avoiding similar disputes in the future

Thus, even minor, insignificant conflicts can be transformed into exercises that improve everyone's skills in listening, collaborative negotiations, and creative problem solving. Each one can deepen our capacity for integrity, patience, compassion, and forgiveness, and increase our ability to learn from our conflicts and transform them into sources of wisdom, insight, and personal and social improvement.

In short, every conflict offers each of its participants an opportunity to overcome what Sigmund Freud called "the narcissism of minor differences" and become better, more balanced, collaborative human beings.

For mediators, a detailed practical and theoretical exploration of how people learn to transform and transcend their conflicts leads to increased effectiveness, even in conflicts that are stuck in impasse or likely to result only in settlement and enduring bitterness. Yet while impasse and settlement can easily be externalized and described objectively, transformation and transcendence are subjective experiences that require us, as mediators, to become fully present and self-aware in order to explore and dismantle our own inherited and instinctual conflict responses. Journeying into the heart of conflicts asks us not simply to become better mediators, but better human beings.

For this reason, at its deeper levels, conflict resolution is naturally and automatically a path of character and integrity, of heart and spirit, that begins here and now inside each of us. In the end, of course, there are no paths. The way forward begins wherever you are, and opens whenever you are ready to open your eyes, drop your judgments and expectations, and act authentically.

More fundamentally, we need to learn how to resolve our differences if we hope to ever end the use of warfare and environmental degradation, or assuage national, religious, and cultural hatreds. This requires us not only to focus our resources on learning and teaching the demanding arts of sciences of dispute resolution, but to recognize that we can only succeed in eliminating war and hatred in others by discovering how to eliminate them in ourselves.

Kenneth Cloke

Kenneth Cloke, J.D., L.L.M., Ph.D., is the director of the Center for Dispute Resolution. He is a mediator, arbitrator, consultant, and trainer to individuals, large organizations, and corporations. He is the author of *Resolving Conflicts at Work, Mediating Dangerously, Resolving Personal and Organizational Conflicts, The Art of Waking People Up, The End of Management, The Dance of Opposites, Conflict Revolution: Mediating Evil, War, Injustice,* and *Terrorism and The Crossroads of Conflict.*

1

What Is Conflict?

Peace is the skillful management of conflict.

KENNETH BOULDING

Two old farmers bought property next to each other. One of the farmer's hens wandered under the fence onto the other farmer's property. After laying an egg, the hen wandered back home. The farmer looked out his window and saw his hen coming back. He went out to the fence and saw the egg. Just as he started to move forward and pick up the egg, the other farmer came to the fence, grabbed the egg, turned, and walked away.

"Excuse me, that's my egg. My hen wandered onto your property and laid that egg."

"I can see that," the other farmer said. "The egg is on my property, so it's now my egg."

"I don't think so," the farmer insisted. "It's my hen, so it's my egg."

"Look, where I come from we have a way to settle disputes. We take turns punching each other in the stomach twenty times. The first one to say 'Uncle' has to let the other person keep the egg."

"That's fair," the farmer with the hen replied. "Let's do it."

The other farmer said, "Okay, I'll go first." He held the egg in one hand and proceeded to punch his neighbor twenty times in the stomach with his other hand. His neighbor groaned and grimaced with every punch, but took all twenty. He took a deep breath and said, "Okay, now it's my turn." He rolled up his sleeves and took a step forward. The farmer with the egg extended his hand with the egg and said, "Uncle! You can have your stupid egg!"

That's not exactly the best way to resolve conflict, but, unfortunately, people don't always resolve conflict in the healthiest manner. What exactly is conflict? Noah Webster defined conflict as:

- Fight; battle; struggle
- Sharp disagreement or opposition, as of interests, ideas, etc.
- Emotional disturbance resulting from a clash of impulses in a person

Other definitions include:

- Competitive or opposing action of incompatibilities
- Antagonistic state or action (as of divergent ideas, interests, or persons)
- Struggle resulting from incompatible needs, drives, wishes or demands
- Hostile encounter

POINT TO PONDER

Conflict alternately strokes and crushes our egos, fuels and exhausts our will, energizes us and freezes us in fear. It speaks to a deep, ancient part of our soul that thirsts for power and delights in revenge.

KENNETH CLOKE

Conflict Comes in Many Forms

To be alive is to face conflict. It begins when we leave our mother's warm and comfortable womb. The doctor swats us on our bottom and we are shocked as we gasp our first breath of air. Various forms of conflict follow us through childhood, adulthood, and on to the grave. It's been suggested that by the time we're in our mid-sixties, we've spent several thousand hours in some form of conflict. It's all part of the human experience.

Conflict is quite normal, natural, and to be expected when people live and work together. It doesn't necessarily mean that one person or a group of people is bad and the other person or group is good. It doesn't mean that the motivations on one side are negative and the other side's are positive. Conflict occurs when people…

- care about an issue.
- disagree about an issue.
- misunderstand each other about an issue.

If you lived on an island by yourself, you could do anything your heart desired. You could run around in your birthday suit in freedom and throw sand into the air. There would be no one to complain about your behavior. But if I moved onto the island with you, there would be conflict. Your freedom ends where my nose begins. I might have different needs, drives, and wishes. I might have a conflict with you on values, beliefs, and interests. As more people move onto the island, there is more potential for conflict.

Conflict may occur when there are unclear jurisdictions of responsibilities and authority. When boundaries are fuzzy, people often wander into other people's territory. Role definitions may overlap. Job descriptions may not be clearly outlined…or followed.

Conflict may occur when two individuals or groups have the same interest in mind. They may need the same resources. The resources may be limited, so one individual or group won't be able to reach their goals.

Conflict may occur when there are communication barriers. There may be little or no communication taking place. This may be caused by time difficulties or the restraint of distance. Communication may simply be unclear so misunderstandings arise.

Conflict may occur when people or groups of people are dependent on others for the accomplishment of their tasks. They must rely on other people's performance. If others don't follow through, the project may be damaged, altered, or uncompleted.

CONFLICT CAUSES

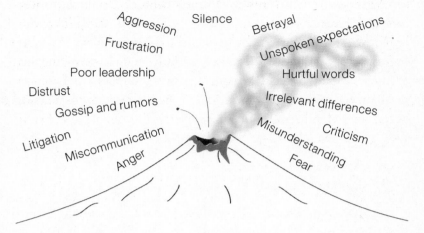

Conflict may occur when different levels of authority are involved. When chain-of-command isn't followed, disruption may occur. Jurisdictional disputes may create many disagreements. Various levels of power may cause tension, fear, and anger.

Conflict may occur when decisions have to be made by a group of people. This type of discussion requires conflict resolution skills. Each of the parties may be at a different level and ability in making decisions and handling disagreements productively.

Conflict may occur when there must be a consensus among the parties involved. It's often difficult to get everyone in a group to agree on a subject or solution. And if the group decides on a particular course of action, not everyone may support the action with full participation.

Conflict may occur when there is an excess of regulations. When rules and regulations are imposed, it's a natural human tendency to rebel or resent those rules. New policies and procedures are seldom received with open arms. Change is difficult for most people. It's been said that the only one who likes change is a newborn baby.

Conflict may occur due to a history of prior unresolved conflicts between the parties. The trust level may be extremely low. People may not want to commit themselves to another situation where they might be hurt or embarrassed. Broken commitments take time to be overcome. A Chinese proverb says, "Trust, like fine china, once broken can be repaired...but it is never quite the same."

Conflict may occur when selfishness is involved. An unwillingness to negotiate, compromise, or work together can turn minor conflicts into war. Individuals are only concerned about their own welfare or interests and destroy family or business unity. The welfare of individuals or groups takes a backseat to their own interests.

POINT TO PONDER

Chronic conflicts are systemic, and all systems, be they personal, familial, relational, organizational, social, economic, or political, defend themselves against change, even when it is essential for their survival. Thus, the greater the need for change and the deeper the potential transformation, the greater the resistance, the more intense the conflict, and the more difficult it becomes to even imagine resolving or letting it go.

KENNETH CLOKE

Conflict may occur when different social styles become frustrated with the behaviors of other social styles. Someone may not be making decisions fast enough for someone else. They may not be thinking through their decisions and realizing the conflict that their fuzzy thinking might cause. Differences in behavior inevitably cause conflict.

Conflict seems to break down into four major areas:

1. Misunderstanding and poor communication of information
2. Diversities of values, goals, expectations, interests, and a multitude of different opinions

3. Competition over time, money, resources, and survival instincts

4. Sinful or socially unacceptable attitudes, habits, words, or behaviors

FOUR TERRIBLE TRUTHS ABOUT CONFLICT

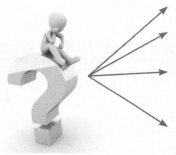

Conflict will happen.

Conflict involves risks, costs, pain, and struggle.

Conflict causes and creates dysfunctional strategies and relationships.

Conflict damage is sometimes irreversible.

As you can see, there are many causes for conflict. There are also many perceptions about conflict. Some people see conflict as negative, while others see it as positive. Your family of origin and past patterns of thinking certainly play roles in how you deal with conflict today.

The goals of this guide are to help you:

- understand what causes conflict
- discover and use conflict-resolution skills
- settle differences and issues constructively
- realize the necessity of forgiveness
- reconcile relationships
- develop effective methods for dealing with future conflicts

First, examine the lists that follow and evaluate your assumptions about conflict.

Your Assumptions About Conflict

In the following two lists, place checks in the boxes that most clearly represent your present views toward conflict.

The Dirty Dozen

- ☐ Anxiety
- ☐ Disagreement
- ☐ Tension
- ☐ Competition
- ☐ Threat
- ☐ Alienation
- ☐ Pain
- ☐ Anger
- ☐ Hostility
- ☐ Destruction
- ☐ Heartache
- ☐ War

The Healthy Dozen

- ☐ Exciting
- ☐ Strengthening
- ☐ Opportunity
- ☐ Enriching
- ☐ Helpful
- ☐ Clarifying
- ☐ Stimulating
- ☐ Courageous
- ☐ Creative
- ☐ Growth producing
- ☐ Learning experience
- ☐ Relationship building

What Is Causing My Conflict?

- ☐ Anger and yelling
- ☐ Child-rearing differences
- ☐ Communication barriers
- ☐ Conflict with peers
- ☐ Delay in decision making
- ☐ Difficulties with relatives
- ☐ Disagreement with boss
- ☐ Failure of others to perform
- ☐ Hurtful comments
- ☐ Lack of spiritual harmony
- ☐ Low trust level
- ☐ Marital arguments
- ☐ Misunderstanding
- ☐ Negative attitude
- ☐ Not keeping commitments

- ☐ Not listening
- ☐ Overspending
- ☐ Physical abuse
- ☐ Procrastination
- ☐ Sarcastic comments
- ☐ Selfishness
- ☐ Silence and shunning
- ☐ Unclear jurisdictions and responsibilities
- ☐ Understaffed and limited resources
- ☐ Unforgiveness
- ☐ Unfounded rumors
- ☐ Unwillingness to negotiate
- ☐ Other _____

The High Price of Conflict

- ☐ Litigation
- ☐ Strikes
- ☐ Reduced productivity
- ☐ Poor morale
- ☐ Wasted time
- ☐ Lost customers
- ☐ Destructive battles
- ☐ Stifling rules
- ☐ Broken relationships
- ☐ Jobs lost
- ☐ Reputations ruined
- ☐ Marriages broken
- ☐ Families destroyed
- ☐ Countries at war

How Were You Taught to Deal with Conflict?

Place a check by familiar phrases from your past.

- ☐ Stop it.
- ☐ Knock it off.
- ☐ Act your age.
- ☐ Life's not fair.
- ☐ Don't hit others.
- ☐ Just ignore them.
- ☐ Stop your fighting.
- ☐ Don't rock the boat.
- ☐ Be a man and fight back.
- ☐ Knock each other silly.
- ☐ You're driving me nuts.
- ☐ You'd better stop it or else.
- ☐ Pick on someone your own size.
- ☐ Stop that or you'll get a spanking.
- ☐ Good boys/girls don't act like that.
- ☐ Nice boys/girls don't say things like that.
- ☐ Don't talk to me like that, young man/young lady.
- ☐ If you can't say anything nice, don't say anything at all.
- ☐ Sticks and stones may break my bones, but names will never hurt me.
- ☐ Other _____

Our past conditioning may play a large role in our conflict resolution skills. If we have been conditioned to think that all conflict is bad and should be avoided, we'll most likely do so. If we've been conditioned to "bite our tongues," we'll often just smile and not say what we really feel.

There are many myths and misconceptions about conflict. In the next section, we'll look at some of these myths and how to recondition our thinking regarding conflict.

POINT TO PONDER

Conflict is a warning light pointing at something in our character, relationship, or environment that is not working, either for ourselves or for others.

KENNETH CLOKE

2

Ten Myths About Conflict

*It is well to remind ourselves that anxiety signifies
a conflict, and so long as a conflict is going
on, a constructive solution is possible.*

ROLLO MAY

When you think of the word "conflict," what comes to mind? For some people, it's a negative situation that should always be avoided. For others, conflict isn't such a bad thing and can result in healthy resolutions. There are many myths about conflict we'll address. Review the following ten myths and evaluate your own beliefs about them. Have you found yourself embracing any of these myths at one time or another?

Myth 1: All Conflict Is Bad

Many people believe conflict is bad because emotions get aroused and issues are often left unsettled. Because they don't like the negative feelings they're dealing with, people tend to avoid conflict. The establishing of the United States began with a conflict between freedom and tyranny. The ending of slavery required a conflict. Standing up to a bully at school to end his or her reign of terror may be unnerving and difficult, but the result will be long-term peace.

Conflict often arises when the rights of one person or a group are violated. Accepting the violation doesn't settle the issue. The violation needs to be discussed and resolved, if possible. This means the conflict might result in positive change. Conflict can increase the motivation of both individuals and groups to learn to get along with each other. Conflict can encourage increased creativity and problem solving. Conflict can help individuals or a group unify as they seek mutual goals. Conflict can lead to understanding and the clearing up of miscommunication. Conflict can also help individuals and people within groups to grow emotionally and spiritually.

Myth 2: Conflict Damages Relationships

It's true that conflict can damage or destroy a relationship. It's also true that conflict can unify a relationship when misunderstandings are cleared up. Resolving conflicts can draw people together. Positive confrontation and conflict resolution dissolves built-up bitterness and paves the way to healthy cohesiveness.

Myth 3: Conflict Should Never Be Escalated

Sometimes conflict must be escalated before a resolution can be reached. The escalation of conflict is a major factor in labor union disputes. When the workforce goes on strike, it helps to force the issue. The increase of conflict becomes so uncomfortable that the individuals or groups have to face each other. They have to work it out. The conflict itself becomes the catalyst that sets in motion needed change.

Myth 4: All Conflicts Are Just Personality Problems

The implied concept is that if you disagree with me, there is something wrong with you. There must be something inherent in your character and personality that isn't operating correctly. This also suggests that the only people who have conflicts are those with personality problems. The fact is, *everyone faces conflicts* or will start conflicts with people. When personality and social style differences enter into situations, the intensity of the conflict increases but it isn't necessarily the cause of the conflict.

POINT TO PONDER

The real reason we believe people or their personalities

are the problem is that we simply do not know what to do to resolve the conflict and have given up trying.

KENNETH CLOKE

Myth 5: Conflict Should Be Reduced or Avoided

Yes, it would be nice if conflict could be reduced or avoided. However, we must keep in mind that conflict is a universal human experience. It's going to come our way whether we like it or not. We'll continue to experience conflicts with our own personality. We won't be able to escape conflicts in our relationships. We can't run from conflicts caused by unforeseen accidents, illnesses, and acts of nature. The best option is to reduce our negative emotional reactions to conflict rather than try to avoid conflict, which is impossible. Let's learn healthy methods for dealing with and resolving conflict.

Myth 6: Conflict Indicates Psychological Problems

There's no question that people with psychological problems have conflicts. But so does everyone else. Those who have psychological issues are sometimes hampered to a greater extent in coping with their problems. They often don't possess the skills necessary to constructively deal with conflict. When conflict occurs, to say it's because an individual has psychological problems is simply a put-down technique. The person making the comment is trying to elevate him- or herself in a "one-upmanship" position. Conflict is normal between all people.

POINT TO PONDER

By defining our opponents as evil, we implicitly define ourselves as good. Our opponents' apparently demonic behaviors allow us to appear—if not angelic by comparison—at least poor, innocent victims who are entitled to sympathy and support.

KENNETH CLOKE

Myth 7: Harmony Is Normal; Conflict Is Abnormal

This myth doesn't even touch reality. It's usually suggested by those who can't or won't deal with conflict. It's not a pleasant experience to confront anyone. When such people find their emotions of anger and fear rising to the surface, it makes them uncomfortable. Rather than facing their emotions (or the emotions of others), they run from conflict. They withdraw, avoid, and shun conflict situations or conflict-producing people. To help avoid their fear, they suggest that harmony is normal and conflict is abnormal. This is used as a technique to get conformity out of others, to get them to change their behavior. You must not be normal if you're involved in conflict. The truth is that harmony *is possible* and conflict is normal.

Myth 8: Conflicts and Disagreements Are the Same Thing

There is a difference between "conflicts" and "disagreements." When conflict occurs, there is usually no communication taking place. People are either attacking one another or withdrawing from one another. With disagreement, discussion is usually happening or at least some form of communication. As long as a disagreement is discussed, there is hope for the conflict coming to some form of resolution.

Myth 9: Genuine Conflict Is About Facts Not Emotions

There are those who endeavor to separate facts from emotions in conflict situations. They suggest that only the facts are important. The implication is that emotions should not be involved—or at least shouldn't carry as much weight. While it's true that conflict occurs over issues and facts, a person's behavior and emotions do play important roles. Emotions indicate the degree of importance the individual feels about the issue at hand. Emotions are the thermometer that indicates the intensity of the conflict.

Dale Carnegie said, "When dealing with people, remember you are not dealing with creatures of logic, but with creatures of emotion, creatures bristling with prejudice, and motivated by pride and vanity."

Myth 10: Conflict Is a Sign People Don't Care

Nothing could be further from the truth. Conflict is a sign that people genuinely care. Their emotional attachment to the issue is a sign they have deep concerns about the problem at hand. Their willingness to confront the issue, knowing it can result in tension, shows they care.

POINT TO PONDER

In conflict, one person is often more emotionally expressive than another, and it is difficult for more than one person to express emotions at a time and still feel heard.

KENNETH CLOKE

Take a moment to evaluate your own paradigm when it comes to conflict. Do you view all conflict as bad? Do you avoid conflict? Do you think people who engage in conflict don't care? A close examination of your belief system will often give you deeper insights into why you approach conflict the way you do.

3

The Many Faces of Conflict

Seventeen years of conflict is a long time. It started a few years after we were married. Like many young couples, we had our struggles financially. Fortunately, we had enough money for a down payment on a home. We were in our house for a few years when an opportunity to increase our income came along.

We had a friend who owned a building company that was growing rapidly. He shared with us that it was a good time to join with him because the housing market was booming. He told us it was a safe investment because our names would be on the land development along with his. And even, if for some reason, the market would slow down, at least we could hold on to the land until the market began to grow again.

After some consideration, we took out a second loan on our home and invested it in his company. And then it happened. He overextended himself in the home building and land development business. We soon realized our investment was in a little danger. However, we knew that not all would be lost because at least our names were on the land title.

Now, you can probably guess the rest. He hadn't been honest with us, and our names weren't registered as owners of the land as he'd indicated. We were devastated. Now we were forced to pay on a first and a second mortgage on our home. This was in addition to raising a family and all that goes along with that responsibility.

Since I didn't believe in bankruptcy, I had to work two jobs to pay for the expenses incurred in our land investment. And I wasn't alone. Many other people were also talked into investing in the same land development project. Over four million dollars was lost because of dishonest commitments and business mismanagement.

It took seventeen years to pay back the second loan on our home. Every month for seventeen years I was reminded of that business conflict with a friend who had misled many people. The principle and interest on the loan ended up costing our family nearly double our original investment. Not only was I harboring ill feelings toward him, but I was also mad at myself for being sucked into such a situation. I often reminded myself of the adage, "If you could kick the person in the pants responsible for most of your trouble, you wouldn't sit for a month."

POINT TO PONDER

We can disagree forever about what happened in the past, or about who said and did what to whom, or who did it first, or who was most at fault. None of this will get us anywhere.

KENNETH CLOKE

Over the years, I've counseled many people who were dealing with disputes and conflicts. I'm reminded of Carl, who worked for a large company. He was one of the executives who was responsible for purchasing products for his organization. Often he would have deadlines that had to be kept to keep customers happy. On many occasions, he would approach the CEO of the company with requests to buy supplies. He would explain to his boss that there was a short time frame to meet the deadline, and he needed the "go ahead" to purchase the items. What frustrated Carl was that his boss would not or could not make a quick decision. Carl asked me, "How do I approach my boss and tell him he's holding up a large area of the business because he can't make a decision? I've mentioned it to him on several occasions, and all there is from his office is silence. What am I supposed to do?"

Another client, Janice, was on the verge of tears as she came into my office. She said, "I know when you get married you not only marry your spouse but you also marry his family. It's the family I'm struggling with. Especially Jose's mother. She's a very strong and highly opinionated woman. At family gatherings, she'll often get upset. She lets everyone know it with her body language and what she says. Everyone is uncomfortable and guarded when she's around. She's constantly putting Jose down in front of people. He's my husband, and I don't like her attacks and negative spirit. I can't take it anymore. I'm about ready to explode and let her have it, but I think she'll just have one of her temper tantrums. If you get on her bad side, she'll just write you off. She's a huge grudge holder. I feel like I would like to move to another city to get away from her."

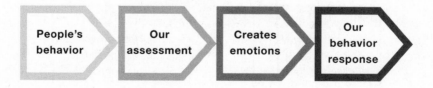

When one of her best friends told her off, Melinda was devastated. She'd been the secretary at a large church when she was approached by several women who admitted having affairs with the pastor. Some of the elders of the church had heard the same information from other sources, so they asked Melinda if she knew anything about the situation. She admitted she did and told the elders what she knew.

At some point, Melinda's best friend discovered that Melinda had talked with the elders. Her friend Cari was furious. Cari was a strong supporter of the pastor and thought that Melinda was just spreading gossip and rumors. Cari unloaded her anger on Melinda. Their relationship was severely damaged.

Later, when it became known to the congregation that the pastor had, indeed, been having a number of affairs, Melinda's role in answering to the elders was justified, but her relationship with Cari wasn't repaired. Melinda was hurt and angry over the unjustified attack by her friend. "I don't know if I can forgive her for the terrible things she said to me."

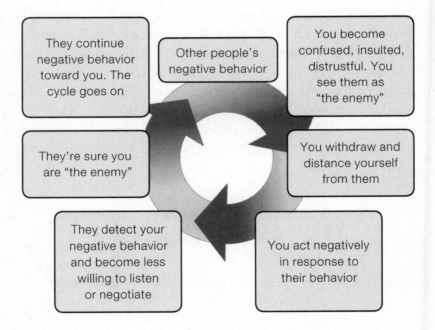

Glen and Sherry had been married for less than a year when they came in for counseling. It was like pulling teeth to get them to share their trouble. Both of them came from family backgrounds where conflict between their parents was never resolved. Everyone in both of their homes hated any form of conflict. No one would deal with any disagreements. They would just become silent and not talk about it. Somehow, they figured, it would eventually go away.

Glen and Sherry carried into their marriage the same modeling they'd learned from their parents. Their silence had grown to such a proportion that they didn't even sleep in the same room. I finally had to see them separately to get to the root of their issues. They couldn't deal with even mild confrontation together.

On the other hand, I'm reminded of Paula and Jason. They were anything but silent. On one occasion, Paula and Jason were at the home of Jason's parents. Something happened where Paula told off Jason's parents in no uncertain terms. She then stormed out, slammed the door, and went home.

Jason's parents said, "You can't let your wife talk to us that way. You're the head of the house." Jason went home. When he came in the door, he yelled, "You can't yell and talk to my parents that way!" Paula proceeded to tell Jason off with even more gusto.

Jason got angry and hauled off and hit Paula in the face. She staggered backward and hit the wall in their dining room. She fell to the floor. She got up and ran into the kitchen, which was next to the dining room. Jason followed quickly after her.

When Jason came around the corner, he slipped and fell on the kitchen floor. It was sort of like a dog coming around a corner with its paws slipping and sliding on the linoleum.

At this point Paula grabbed a butcher knife and jumped onto Jason's chest. She put the knife to his throat, drawing a little blood from the point. "You move, you bleep, bleep, bleep, and I'll kill you."

Paula was quite capable of doing what she threatened to do. It was one of the first times in their marriage where there was very clear communication.

Conflict can come from your spouse, your children, your parents, your relatives, your close friends, and your acquaintances. It can expand to your neighbors, your boss, your fellow workers. Even store clerks, police, or crazy drivers on the road generate situations for tension. You can even experience *intrapersonal* conflict, where you're not happy with your own thinking, emotions, or behavior.

Conflict can arise from natural causes, such as fire, flood, earthquakes, and tornados. Health issues, accidents, and drunk drivers create situations that are difficult to live with. Various forms of crime give rise to conflicting experiences.

FBI CRIME CLOCK

Violent crime
every 25.3 seconds

One murder
every 35.6 minutes

One robbery
every 1.4 minutes

One car theft
every 42.8 seconds

Property crime
every 3.5 seconds

One rape
every 6.2 minutes

One burglary
every 14.6 seconds

One larceny theft
every 5.1 seconds

One aggravated assault
every 40.5 seconds

Conflict can lead to anger, fear, bitterness, resentment, and emotional and physical abuse. Sometimes conflict is used as a smokescreen to hide our weaknesses. We use conflict to divert people away from our poor behavior. In conflict we can blame others and not accept responsibility for our actions. Conflict helps us believe we are on the righteous side of the issue at hand.

POINT TO PONDER

Conflict makes us feel righteous by encouraging us to believe we are opposing evil behaviors and rewarding those that are good. Our opponents' pernicious actions justify us in giving them what they "rightly deserve."

KENNETH CLOKE

We can use conflict to give us "the right" to be angry, retaliate, and get even. Or conflict can help us grow in empathy, honesty, and acceptance. Each conflict we work to resolve gives us more skills for handling future conflicts.

POINT TO PONDER

Holding on to a painful past merely draws it into the present; reduces the likelihood of having a different future; and denies you resolution, closure, and inner peace.

KENNETH CLOKE

4

Ways to View Conflict

*Begin challenging your own assumptions. Your
assumptions are your windows on the world. Scrub them
off every once in a while, or the light won't come in.*

ALAN ALDA

I just can't believe my mother wouldn't come to my daughter's birthday party. She said it was because I didn't call her last week. Ever since Dad died, she's become more and more difficult to get along with. If you don't do something her way or meet her expectations, she tries to punish you by holding back her love or involvement. It's so childish."

Kim spent half an hour describing her relationship with her mother. She expressed frustration and anger over her mother's demanding and immature behavior. This wasn't the first time Kim had to deal with the issues of manipulation and withholding affection. During most of her childhood her mother had acted this way.

Kim is experiencing deep hurt. The emotion of hurt comes with loss or injury. When hurt isn't expressed, it leaves the pain inside. People who are hurt feel victimized, cheated, used, disappointed, overwhelmed, sorrowful, frustrated, and angry. They must discover what their loss means. This is the first step in overcoming the pain of hurt. A good question to ask yourself when you feel the pain of hurt is, "What have I lost?"

"I hate you! I hate you!" I used to say that to my brother. My mother would interrupt. "Now, Robert, don't say you hate your brother. You can say you dislike him, but never say you hate him."

Well, the fact of the matter was I hated my brother. I thought he was mean to me. When he hogtied me in the backyard and left me tied up all afternoon, I thought that was mean. When he and his friends would hold me down, pull up my shirt, and rub grass all over me to make me itch, I thought that was mean. When they buried me up to my waist in the backyard and left me there, I thought that was mean. I longed for the day I could beat my brother up. I longed for the day I could get revenge for all of his meanness toward me.

Have you been hurt by someone and wanted to get even? Have you felt that what was happening to you wasn't fair? You may have come from a dysfunctional home where you had an alcoholic parent. You may have a parent or relative who was physically, emotionally, or sexually abusive toward you. You may have brothers or sisters you didn't get along with or coworkers who treated you unfairly or made fun of you.

Maybe you now have an employer who's hard-nosed and difficult to get along with. Or maybe your marriage is filled with hostility and anger. You may have been the victim of a robbery, assault, or rape. A member of your family may have been killed by a drunk driver. You may have lost money in the stock market or in a "sure thing" land investment like my wife and I did.

Hurt and loss are common in this life. No relationships are without tension at some point. You can't live in a community of people without experiencing conflicts. In fact, in any human relationship, you're exposed to the possibility of experiencing pain, injury, suffering, and alienation.

POINT TO PONDER

We have described our opponents in terms of evil, injustice, unfairness, harassment, aggression, dishonesty, betrayal, and insanity, as opposed to describing our relationship with them in terms of misunderstandings, false expectations, miscommunications, and petty incidents that have been blown out of proportion by both sides.

KENNETH CLOKE

All of us tend to assign blame to someone or something else. When we're hurt by others, whether they yell or are silent, we avoid them. Sometimes we pretend the problem doesn't exist and revert to denial. Often we resent those who we feel have done us wrong.

Are there people in your life you're avoiding? When you see them at a distance, do you cross the street or turn a corner to prevent an encounter? When you're at a social gathering, do you engage in conversation with others so you won't have to face the ones you're in conflict with or talk with them? Do you get a sick feeling in your stomach when you have to communicate with them? Do you basically feel uncomfortable in their presence or even when you hear others talking about them? If so, what's going on? Have you been hurt? Is there a damaged relationship? Are you fearful or angry? Are you filled with resentment toward them? Do you need to forgive them? Do you need to restore and reconcile your relationships?

As I've mentioned, I longed for the day I could get even with my brother. Then one day the opportunity came. When I was older and much larger, my brother began to push me around and "wrestle" with me. Little did he know that he was tapping into twenty years of built-up rage. With the strength of resentment and the desire for revenge, I threw my brother to the ground and injured him. I suddenly realized the hollowness of revenge. I felt terrible. I had dropped to his level—and perhaps then some.

To some people, conflict is negative, fearful, and distasteful. It reeks of betrayal, hurtful words, mistrust, and misunderstanding. Thoughts of distrust, aggression, and litigation lurk in the background. Others see conflict as a positive. Disputes are viewed as a normal part of life and as opportunities for growth and restoration of relationships. To them, conflict is part of the journey of the human experience. They view conflict as a request for communication.

Numerous factors contribute to any conflict. Everyone in the conflict has their own ideas, emotions, attitudes, and intentions about the issue that's causing a dispute. You've heard it takes "two to tango." In the case of conflict, it takes at least two individuals or two groups (sometimes called factions) to make a conflict. Of course, there can be

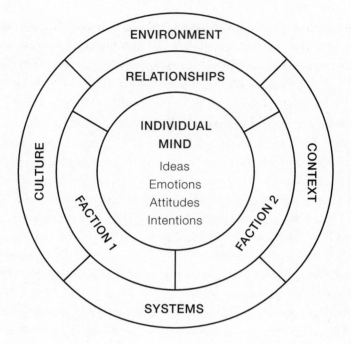

internal conflicts within one individual. An example of this inward individual struggle is mentioned in the Bible, in Romans 7:15-23:

> I don't understand myself at all, for I really want to do what is right, but I can't. I do what I don't want to—what I hate. I know perfectly well that what I am doing is wrong, and my bad conscience proves that I agree with these laws I am breaking. But I can't help myself because I'm no longer doing it. It is sin inside me that is stronger than I am that makes me do these evil things.

> I know I am rotten through and through so far as my old sinful nature is concerned. No matter which way I turn I can't make myself do right. I want to but I can't. When I want to do good, I don't; and when I try not to do wrong, I do it anyway. Now if I am doing what I don't want to, it is plain where the trouble is: sin still has me in its evil grasp.

> It seems to be a fact of life that when I want to do what is

right, I inevitably do what is wrong. I love to do God's will so far as my new nature is concerned; but there is something else deep within me, in my lower nature, that is at war with my mind and wins the fight and makes me a slave to the sin that is still within me. In my mind I want to be God's willing servant, but instead I find myself still enslaved to sin.

So you see how it is: my new life tells me to do right, but the old nature that is still inside me loves to sin. Oh, what a terrible predicament I'm in! Who will free me from my slavery to this deadly lower nature? Thank God! It has been done by Jesus Christ our Lord. He has set me free.

Our individual ideas, emotions, and attitudes are influenced by the culture and family of origin we come from. Some cultures display much emotion in their interactions with each other. There are also cultures that display little emotion and spend most of their conversations discussing facts and details.

The context of a situation also influences what people say and how they act. We often talk and act differently at work than we do at home. A man might say some unkind and cruel things to his family that he would never say to his boss. The reason is that the boss could fire him. The family doesn't have the control or the option to fire the father.

Environment also plays a factor in conflict discussions. The environment could include whether we're inside or outside a building. In some cases, it might not be advisable to have heavy emotional talks where other people might hear what is being shared. Conversely, it might be good to go for a walk and settle issues where privacy is important. Sitting in the hot sun or shivering on a cold park bench on a winter's day might have a negative effect on communication.

The environment could also include the emotional presence. Are the individuals emotionally in a good place for a heavy discussion? Timing is an important issue. Most family arguments occur a half hour before dinner. This is because of poor timing. Everyone is tired from the day, and everyone is hungry. Blood sugar levels are low, and emotional resistance is down. People have to get dinner ready, homework done, and there may be evening meetings that need to be attended. It's not a good time to start a heavy confrontation.

The second most popular time for family arguments is a half hour before everyone leaves home for school and work. Someone may have gotten up late. Lunches need to be made, and everyone has to get dressed and be ready to go. All the family members are under the pressure of time deadlines. This also is not a good time to start a heavy confrontation.

The same is true in a work or social setting. Outside pressures and demands on individuals have a tendency to make them edgy. If the timing is off for the person being confronted, there may be more intense negativity.

There are occasions when married couples need to talk through heavy issues in their relationship. When is a good time for this type of discussion? Before nine o'clock at night. After nine, difficult discussions have a tendency to go downhill. This is because both people are most likely tired and have many things on their agendas for the next day. Because of past experience, they know their issue will probably not be resolved quickly. With that thought in mind, the discussion gets started on a negative note.

For important marriage discussions, plan ahead. Farm your children out to some friends or neighbors. If that can't be done, say to your children, "Your mom and I are going to have a fight." Or you may prefer to say a "heavy discussion." Yes, I'm advocating saying that to the children. Do you think they don't know you argue with each other? It would probably be healthy for them to see their parents working through conflict and coming to a resolution. Have you ever thought that you are role models for conflict resolution to your family? Who is going to teach them if you don't?

If an issue can't be resolved within an hour to an hour and a half, you might want to table it for another time. The reason most counseling sessions only last an hour is that people tend to start repeating themselves after that. So agree on another time, and take a break. This way you can approach the issue with a fresh body and fresh thinking.

Other factors that affect conflict resolution are family systems and organizational systems. In some family systems, everyone yells. In others, everyone keeps silent. In some, there are combinations where some yell and some withdraw. When silent people become yellers or yellers become silent, it throws the family system into disarray. When the family system isn't operating in the normal way, the other members may overreact and try to gain control. They'll become stronger in their yelling or more determined to keep silent and withdraw and shun the outspoken individual.

Culture, context, environment, and systems merge together with the individual's ideas, emotions, attitudes, and intentions. They are part of the conflict atmosphere and must be considered when attempting to settle disputes and manage conflicts.

Bruce was the founding CEO of a mid-sized furniture company. He grew the business from a small staff of 3 to more than 150. He was the face of the business for 30 years. About 10 years into the business, he incorporated and went public. This move created a board of directors to oversee the corporation. Bruce was in the "A" position in the diagram.

Most of the time, Bruce got along well with the board of directors. The board was "B" in the diagram. As the years progressed, Bruce and the board began to have disagreements about the direction the corporation was moving. On a number of occasions, there were strong arguments. Bruce wanted to go one way, but the board had a different path in mind. Finally, Bruce couldn't take it any longer. He made strong statements saying he was the founder and the board had to follow him. The board thought otherwise. The end result was the board gave Bruce the "golden handshake" and let him go.

UNDERSTANDING CONFLICT

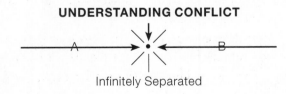

Infinitely Separated

Bruce was devastated. After all his years of service this is what he got. He was hurt, angry, and resentful. He wouldn't talk to the board members, even in social settings. His resentment and bitterness grew and infected his family. They took up the banner of his maltreatment and talked to as many people as they could about the unfairness done to Bruce and their dissatisfaction with the board.

On a number of occasions, the various board members kindly reached out to Bruce, but he would have none of it. After his dismissal, he lived with unforgiveness in his heart. He had no desire for reconciliation in any form. He wasted his later years in bitterness and hostility. Bruce and the board were infinitely separated.

One of the goals of conflict resolution is to attempt to bridge the gap between party "A" and party "B." The bridging of the gap is done by clearing up confusion, misunderstandings, and misinterpretations.

To grasp a full understanding of what is going on, it's important to realize that conflict has at least six major parts: physical, mental, emotions, spiritual, heart, and culture. These six parts are involved in any conflict to some degree. Sometimes the emphasis of the conflict may be displayed through emotional outbursts. Or the conflict might center more on facts, details, laws, and regulations, emphasizing mental capacity. The stress of the conflict might find its focus in physical weariness, ulcers, sleeplessness, or headaches. In rare cases, stress might be displayed in physical fights and out-of-control emotions that lead to extreme violence.

UNDERSTANDING CONFLICT

A ⟶ Communication to bridge the gap ⟵ B

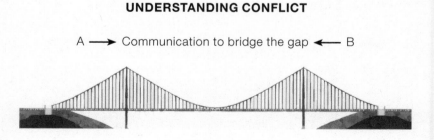

Often, the spiritual component of conflict is overlooked. People forget or don't want to demonstrate kindness, graciousness, love, forgiveness, and other fruit of the Holy Spirit (Galatians 5:22-23). Negative attitudes, lack of trust, and close-mindedness are issues of the heart. This is often shown in rejection, resentment, bitterness, malice, and hatred. Heart issues are closely tied and intertwined with spiritual issues. Cultural backgrounds often add uniqueness to conflict. Organizational factors and personal social styles may either assist or hamper clear communication.

UNDERSTANDING CONFLICT

A Shock

Our heads jerked when we heard the screech of brakes. We looked up just in time to see an incredible scene. The driver of the noisy car threw open his door and jumped out while the car was still moving. He tossed himself on the street in front of an oncoming truck.

There was another screech of brakes. The quick-thinking truck driver somehow got his truck stopped just inches before running over the man who had leaped from the car.

The man on the pavement jumped up and ran down the alley by our office.

The woman who had been riding in the car slid over to the driver's seat of the rolling vehicle. She drove down the alley, pursuing the man who was running away.

My client and I ran out of the office to see what was happening and if there was anything we could do. We wanted to get the license number of the car. By the time we got to the alley, however, the car was too far away.

We looked at each other. We'd just witnessed an attempted suicide.

It takes a great deal of stress and conflict in a person's life to bring him or her to the point of suicide. The fast pace of today's society and the complexity of our lifestyles create much tension. The strain of daily living in a rapidly changing world create tremendous pressure. The name of the game is still survival, but the rules and complexity of life have changed dramatically. To many people, it feels like someone has pushed the fast-forward button on life.

"I want the merry-go-round to stop. I can't take it anymore. Just when I start to get ahead, someone in the family gets sick. Last week a crazy driver ran into my car. He didn't have insurance. And on top of all that, my boss just told me that in the next layoff, I'm the low man on the totem pole. Will it ever end?" Art collapsed into a chair in my office.

Karen said, "I can't keep up with the pressure. My daily schedule is so full I think I'm going to explode." She began to cry. Karen was a working mother with three children. "I don't have any energy left. After I make breakfast, fix the lunches, go to work, pick up the kids after soccer practice, make dinner, wash the dishes, and put in a load of clothes, I can hardly stand up. My husband, Jim, works all day and then goes to night school. He's trying to learn some computer skills so he can get a promotion. We hardly see each other anymore. There must be more to life than this."

Stress and various forms of conflict situations have a way of building up and leaking out into our bodies and our interactions with others. Check the various signs of stress that may be found in your life at this time. This will alert you to any physical effects of stress and conflict you may be experiencing.

Mood Signs of Conflict and Stress

☐ Boredom   ☐ Depression
☐ Confusion   ☐ Detachment

- ☐ Disorientation
- ☐ Escape thoughts
- ☐ Feeling low
- ☐ Forgetfulness
- ☐ Impatience
- ☐ Insecurity
- ☐ Irritability
- ☐ Listlessness

- ☐ Nervousness
- ☐ Overexcitement
- ☐ Paranoia
- ☐ Quick-temperedness
- ☐ Sadness
- ☐ Sleep loss
- ☐ Uneasiness
- ☐ Worry

Visceral Signs of Conflict and Stress

- ☐ Cold chills
- ☐ Cold hands
- ☐ Colitis
- ☐ Cramps
- ☐ Diarrhea
- ☐ Dry mouth
- ☐ Fainting

- ☐ Heartburn
- ☐ Heart pounding
- ☐ Lightheadedness
- ☐ Moist hands
- ☐ Nausea
- ☐ Sweating
- ☐ Ulcers

Musculoskeletal Signs of Conflict and Stress

- ☐ Arthritis
- ☐ Back pain
- ☐ Cramps
- ☐ Fidgeting
- ☐ Fist clenching
- ☐ Grinding teeth
- ☐ Headaches

- ☐ Jaw tightening
- ☐ Shaky hands
- ☐ Stiff neck
- ☐ Stuttering
- ☐ Tense muscles
- ☐ Tics
- ☐ Twitches

Other Signs of Conflict and Stress

- ☐ Cold sores
- ☐ Compulsiveness
- ☐ Exhaustion
- ☐ Low spiritual life
- ☐ Nail biting
- ☐ Neglecting family

- ☐ Fatigue
- ☐ Frequent colds
- ☐ Hair-twisting
- ☐ Hay fever
- ☐ Heart disease
- ☐ High alcohol use

- ☐ High caffeine use
- ☐ High nicotine use
- ☐ High sugar use
- ☐ Jumpiness
- ☐ Low sex drive
- ☐ Neglecting friends

The basic reactions to conflict and stress are either flight or fight. The individual may resist or do away with conflict or he or she may run and escape from it. The response will vary depending on the circumstances. Sometimes it's the best course of action to stand up to a bully who is pushing you around. You may need to face the conflict and teach the person you aren't afraid and that the person can't get his or her way all the time. On the other hand, when the bully has his or her entire gang for support and your life may be in the balance, escape may be the proper response. You may save yourself by the quick reaction of turning and running away.

FLIGHT   **FIGHT**

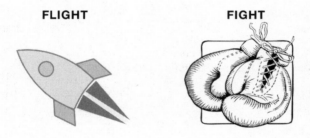

There are three stages to stress: alarm, resistance, and exhaustion. In the alarm stage, the body is alerted to the need for action. Adrenaline flows and the body responds. The next stage is resistance. This is the "fight or flight" response. However, the body can only fight or flee for so long. It will eventually run out of energy. This leads to the exhaustion stage.

Too little stress encourages laziness, apathy, boredom, and dullness. We need some *healthy stress* to develop positivity, productivity, fun, and excitement in our lives. If we get an overabundance of stress, we become *unproductive*. Our bodies are always on the alert for feelings of discomfort, concern, and pressure. If conflict and stress are chronic and last for a long period, they become *unhealthy stress*. We begin to feel strain and experience burnout. This can, and often does, lead to illness and even death.

There will always be some degree of conflict and stress in our lives. We need to make peace with the fact that conflict is part of the human experience. And since we can't live our lives stress free or conflict free, we'll explore some skills for dealing with people and uncomfortable situations.

CONFLICT AND STRESS CYCLE

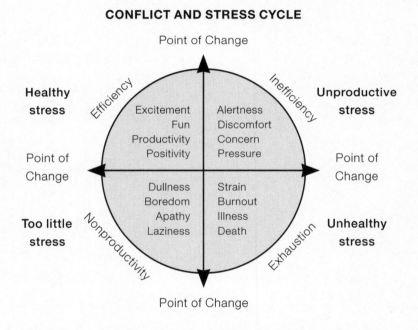

POINT TO PONDER

Sweet are the uses of adversity,
Which, like the toad, ugly and venomous,
Wears yet a precious jewel in his head.

WILLIAM SHAKESPEARE,
AS YOU LIKE IT, ACT 2, SCENE 1

5

Dealing with Conflict
Mentally and Emotionally

The time to win a fight is before it starts.

FREDERICK W. LEWIS

I t's all in your mind." Have you ever had someone say that to you? "You're making a mountain out of a molehill." Has that remark been mentioned to you? Sometimes we create or escalate a potential conflict in our minds. We jump to conclusions or we make assumptions. As a result, conflict brews inside our heads before we have a chance to think through all the facts.

Sometimes emotions get in the way. We allow past experiences to frame the outcome of potential conflict. Once the feelings and actual facts of the conflict are mingled in our minds, behaviors manifest. Some of those behaviors include withdrawing, acting aggressive, competing, debating, and problem solving. As the flow-chart depicts, conflict begins with circumstances, comments, or behaviors, and progresses to either agreement or defeat. As you equip yourself with the necessary tools to deal with conflict, you'll be able to transition from unproductive, defeating conflict to productive conflict solutions. The process of dealing with conflict mentally and emotionally can be best addressed with the methods that follow.

Method 1: Get More Information Before You Respond

When a conflicting event occurs, a person can sometimes perceive or assume that certain things are happening when they really aren't. We

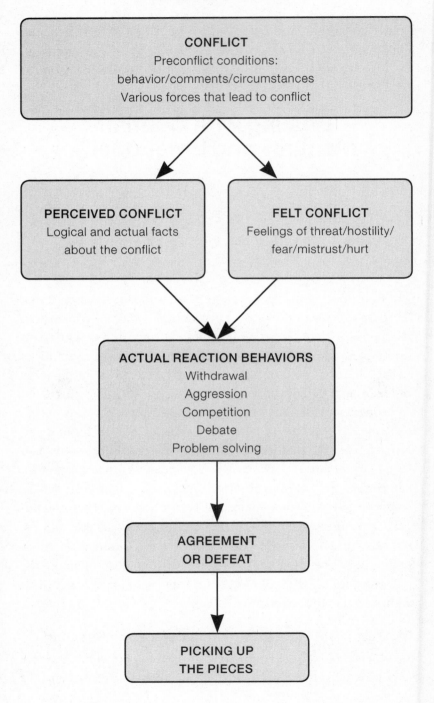

need to get more information to determine if the way we're feeling or thinking is based on valid reasons or not. We may not have gotten all the facts. We may have misunderstood what someone said. A friend or coworker may have given us false information.

Before we lash out verbally at someone, we'd do well to ask a few questions. Questions are a great way to get more information and clarify other people's words and actions without intensifying the situation. Consider such questions as:

- I'm not sure I understood what you meant. Will you please explain it a little more?

- I get the impression you're upset with me. Are you?

- I noticed you were doing _____. Will you please help me understand why you were doing that?

- I may be wrong, but I feel as though there may be a problem between us. Is my perception correct?

POINT TO PONDER

To answer before listening—that is folly and shame.

PROVERBS 18:13 NIV

As you can see by the following Flow of Conflict chart, conflict interrupts an otherwise tranquil existence. We may be on cruise control in life when some form of conflict triggers a reaction. The first process in coping with the conflict is the mental response. A verbal response often follows, as well as a physical response. The mental, verbal, and physical responses can all be negative responses or positive ones, depending on the choices we exercise.

Method 2: Go to the Memory File

When you feel yourself getting upset over some conflicting event, be

THE FLOW OF CONFLICT

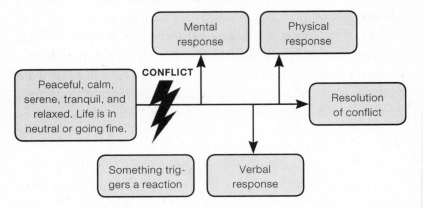

sure to make a stop at the "memory file." Does the individual involved in the conflict remind you of someone out of your past? It might be a parent, relative, or friend. It might be a former boss, teacher, or someone in authority. The situation you presently face might remind you of a previous conflict. It might be very similar. It's important *not* to bring feelings and emotions out of the past and add them to your present situation. As you review your memory files, you may be surprised how much hurt, anger, and old grudges you carry with you, ready to deposit into a new situation.

POINT TO PONDER

"The horror of that moment," the King went on, "I shall never, never forget!"

"You will, though," the Queen said, "if you don't make a memorandum of it."

LEWIS CARROLL, *ALICE IN WONDERLAND*

Method 3: Become Aware of the "Displacement Response"

Many conflict situations can find their roots in the displacement of emotions. People can be upset or angry with one person and take it out on somebody else. We all have experienced having a bad day and taking out our frustrations on our family and friends.

Have you found yourself pressing harder on the gas pedal after someone cut you off on the freeway? Do you tickle your children unmercifully? Have you found yourself playing roughly with your dog on occasion? Are you short on patience at times? If so, you may be displacing your emotions.

Method 4: Evaluate Your Feelings

Stopping for a moment to evaluate your feelings can be very wise. Make some notes and list the people or things that annoy you. Have you been hurt by something someone said? Have you been jumping to conclusions about your situation and looking at worst case scenarios? Are you feeling threatened or inferior? Look for patterns of recurring emotions in your life.

Have you ever driven down the road or stopped at a red light and realized you were talking to yourself? You were thinking about something and experiencing strong emotions—strong enough to talk out loud to yourself or to the person you were thinking about. Consider putting your thoughts "on trial." Is what you're thinking about based on facts or feelings? What is the source of those thoughts or facts? Is it reliable? Is it biased?

As you mentally face conflict, you'll experience initial feelings in response to the conflict. These first feelings let you know there is an issue that needs to be addressed and how important it is to you. The following chart shows many initial feelings you may experience in response to conflict.

POINT TO PONDER

Anger is never sudden. It is born of a long, prior irritation that has ulcerated the spirit and built up an accumulation of force that results in an explosion. It follows that a fine outburst of rage is by no means a sign of a frank, direct nature.

CESARE PAVESE

WHAT ARE YOUR FIRST FEELINGS?

ANGER

- ☐ Annoyed
- ☐ Frustrated
- ☐ Irritated
- ☐ Disgusted
- ☐ Resentful
- ☐ Hostile

EVENT ⟶ CONFUSION   OR ANY COMBINATION

- ☐ Nervous
- ☐ Dismayed
- ☐ Perplexed
- ☐ Untrusting
- ☐ Exasperated
- ☐ Distressed

FEAR

- ☐ Apprehensive
- ☐ Discouraged
- ☐ Sad
- ☐ Anxious
- ☐ Worried
- ☐ Panic-stricken

As you examine your feelings, there are a few questions you may want to ask yourself. Are you focusing on the positive or the negative? Are you thinking about what's going right in your life or on all the things that can go wrong? Are you becoming anxious, fearful, and worried? Are you finding yourself angry, resentful, and full of hate? What are the advantages and disadvantages of continuing to think along these lines? Listen to your feelings. They're letting you know how important this event is to you.

The apostle Paul talked about having a positive attitude in all things:

Always be full of joy in the Lord; I say it again, rejoice! Let everyone see that you are unselfish and considerate in all you do. Remember that the Lord is coming soon. Don't worry about anything; instead, pray about everything; tell God your needs, and don't forget to thank him for his answers. If you do this, you will experience God's peace, which is far more wonderful than the human mind can understand. His peace will keep your thoughts and your hearts quiet and at rest as you trust in Christ Jesus.

And now, brothers, as I close this letter, let me say this one more thing: Fix your thoughts on what is true and good and right. Think about things that are pure and lovely, and dwell on the fine, good things in others. Think about all you can praise God for and be glad about. Keep putting into practice all you learned from me and saw me doing, and the God of peace will be with you (Philippians 4:4-9).

This might be the time to start thinking new thoughts rather than continue any negative self-talk. When was the last time you looked for the truth and a more honorable way of thinking? How often do you seek that which is "true and good and right"? Have you developed the habit of finding positive character traits in others? Are there things you should be thankful for? As your attitude gradually changes, you'll experience more peace and tranquility—even in the midst of trials.

Remember, there is a difference between "problems" and "facts of life." Problems are situations you have the ability to work on and change. If you have a flat tire, you can fix it. If you need an education, you can go to school. If you're out of work, you can seek employment. If you have a conflict with someone, you can work on it. Charles Swindoll suggested that only ten percent of life is what happens to you. The other ninety percent is how you choose to react to it.

Facts of life are situations over which you have no control. You have no control over the drunk driver who kills your child. You have no control over an earthquake that destroys your house. You have no control over coming down with cancer. Those things happen to the best and the worst of people. In those cases, you must make peace with pain. They aren't something to get fearful or angry over. That won't change a thing. Prayer, acceptance, palliative treatments, and sometimes resignation are the courses of action that will bring peace. While you may not be able to control everything that happens to you, what you *can* control is how you respond.

French writer Francois Fenelon suggested that "if we recognize the hand of God and make no opposition in our will, we have comfort in our affliction. Happy, indeed, are these who can bear their sufferings in the enjoyment of this simple peace and perfect submission to the will of God! Nothing so shortens and soothes our pains as this spirit of non-resistance." How are you responding to the difficulties and conflicts in your life? At the end of this chapter is a worksheet you can copy and use to help you evaluate conflicts, your emotional responses, and how you might want to proceed to handle the situation.

POINT TO PONDER

There are three essential steps you will need to complete closure:

First—you will need to be willing to acknowledge your own role in the conflict.

Second—you will need to be willing to recognize your opponent as a human being.

Third—you will need to forgive your opponent and yourself.

KENNETH CLOKE

Situation Evaluation Worksheet

Conflict situation

Trigger event

My initial thoughts

My initial emotions

My initial physical responses

My initial reaction was:

☐ Flight: Withdraw / Escape / Run away / Become silent
☐ Fight: Stand my ground / Be bold and aggressive / Be outspoken

Is this event similar to another event in my life?

☐ Yes   ☐ No

If yes, what event?

I need to get more information and clarification about:

What would you like to do about this event or situation?

- ☐ Remain upset and angry
- ☐ Harbor bitterness, resentment, and hatred
- ☐ Get even, get revenge
- ☐ Clear up misunderstandings
- ☐ Settle issues
- ☐ Seek or give forgiveness
- ☐ Make restitution
- ☐ Become reconciled and be on good terms again
- ☐ Learn conflict resolution skills to prevent recurrence of this type of conflict

What will you **choose** *to do about this event or situation?*

6

What's the Issue?

A mother can't seem to get her teenaged daughter to obey the rules. The daughter rebels and doesn't come home when she should. The mother continues to yell at her and to send her to her room. The cycle continues because no one seems to know how to get to the heart of the issue.

An employee hates his boss. He loathes coming to work in the morning, and his attitude is slowly worsening. His boss feels like every effort has been made to solve the problem, but he's not exactly sure what the real issue is. The employee has never taken the time to pinpoint what the real trouble is either.

The city council meetings seem to be getting more tense every month. Conflict abounds, and the town appears to be polarized. When one group supports a project, the other group inevitably opposes it. The verbal bashings at the microphone escalate as each side states their views. As emotions escalate, everyone seems to lose sight of what the real issues are.

The nation seems to be more and more divided as each year passes. Republicans and Democrats continue to argue over issues that are emotionally volatile and extremely heated. As the debates escalate, the real issues are often neglected as emotions rise. Each side is very passionate about their views and willing to take a strong stand on what they feel is important for the nation and what is not.

One country values democracy while another maintains the value of autocratic rule. Other countries step forward with their own values and beliefs and join in the conflict. As the tensions grow and countries maintain their willingness to fight and die for what they value, war talk begins. Oftentimes there are more issues than one on the line when conflicts escalate to fighting. Identifying all of those issues and finding agreement on what the issues really are isn't easy. In fact, sometimes it's downright impossible.

Identifying Conflict

The level of conflict you may face will vary from mild to extreme. Have you ever been in the midst of a conflict and lost sight of what the real issue was? Maybe you were never really sure of what the true issue was in the first place. True conflict resolution requires that you focus on the actual issue and then find viable solutions to solve the problem.

Conflict can exist at a minor level on a minor issue or it can exist on a large-scale level on a major issue. Conflict can fall somewhere in-between as well. Focusing on understanding what the particular conflict is all about can be done by looking at five major areas of conflict. Check *one* box that most generally represents a current conflict you're facing. Generally, as conflict moves from intrapersonal to intergroup, it becomes more severe.

FIVE ELEMENTS IN ALL CONFLICTS

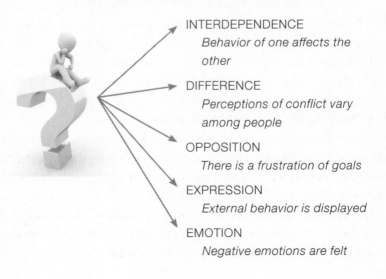

INTERDEPENDENCE
Behavior of one affects the other

DIFFERENCE
Perceptions of conflict vary among people

OPPOSITION
There is a frustration of goals

EXPRESSION
External behavior is displayed

EMOTION
Negative emotions are felt

Peace

ESCALATING CONFLICT — ONSET AREA

☐ **Intrapersonal**

This area involves conflicts and personal problems that an individual has within his or her own life. Examples include low self-image, shyness, pride, lack of patience, quick temper, depression, and anxiety.

☐ **Interpersonal**

This area involves conflicts between two people. It could be between husband and wife, employer and employee, parent and child, relative and relative, friend and friend, or stranger and stranger.

☐ **Small Group**

This area involves small groups of people who are at variance with each other. It could include interoffice departments, church groups, community groups, and competitors in business and educational institutions.

☐ **Large Group**

This area involves conflict with collections of people, such as Republicans versus Democrats, federal employees versus private business employees, state workers versus union employees. It might include state rights advocates versus federal rights advocates.

☐ **Intergroups**

This area involves conflict on a grand scale. This could include one country against another country. It could be a group of countries against another group of countries.

War

Escalating Conflict Levels

Once you've determined where your conflict resides, you can focus on pinpointing the real issues. This is the process of finding the issue *without* focusing on the emotions. Are you dealing with a space conflict or a schedule conflict? Is the conflict related to methods or procedures? Is it a result of personal preferences, traditions, customs, values, or beliefs? In the chart on the next page, check the box that most represents the specific conflict you are currently facing.

☐ **Space**

This refers to an infringement of one's physical space, responsibilities, or area of supervision.

☐ **Schedules**

This refers to a conflict of individual schedules and deadlines between two people or between groups of people.

☐ **Methods**

This refers to how individual people approach the task. Not everyone works at the same pace or has the same idea as to how a task should be accomplished.

☐ **Procedures**

This refers to a set of established forms or methods for conducting business. There is often disagreement regarding these steps and the course of action to be taken.

☐ **Personal Preference**

This refers to personal taste, style, or opinion regarding how a task should be done and the time it will take.

☐ **Traditions**

This refers to a body of unwritten precepts that have been time honored within the group or organization. To violate these traditions might threaten some people in the group.

☐ **Customs**

This refers to a long-established practice or duty carried out by individuals within a group. This habitual practice often has the force of law or censure.

☐ **Values**

This refers to strongly held ideals, principles, and standards that are highly prized by the individual or the group. People are willing to "go to war" over the things they value.

☐ **Beliefs**

This refers to strongly held convictions by the individual or the group. The individual or group is willing to die for what they believe.

Fight to the death

Levels of Conflict

As you discover what the issue really is, you'll also discover there are various levels of conflict. Conflict may start as a mere difference of opinion, which can be categorized as a "spat." A spat normally leads to confrontation. If escalated and unresolved, the spat can lead to a heated debate or argument. This can be categorized as a "quarrel." This level of conflict often leads to division. If escalated further and left unresolved, it can lead to intense physical anger, which can result in a "fight." This often results in rejection. On a large-scale level, when this further escalates to having the hostility confirmed, it leads to "war," which results in ultimate separation.

VARIOUS LEVELS OF CONFLICT

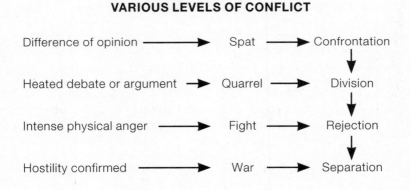

Once you've pinpointed the real issue, you can take steps to resolve the conflict. Whether the conflict is on an interpersonal level or at an intragroup level, the real issue must be examined before resolution can ensue. The next chapter provides three basic approaches to resolving conflicts.

POINT TO PONDER

Research on problem-solving indicates that the effectiveness of solutions increases 85 percent once the true problem has been identified. For these reasons, consider spending most of your time identifying and analyzing the problem. Resolution will emerge effortlessly once a well–defined problem has been mutually identified by all interested parties.

KENNETH CLOKE

7

Three Approaches to Resolving Conflict

Conflict resolution requires energy, wisdom, and creativity.

I've had just about enough of your mouth, young man!" Patrick stood up and moved closer to his fifteen-year-old stepson, Jimmy. "Your constant rebellion and disrespect for your mother is going to stop, and it's going to stop now."

The conflict had been building for months. Jimmy was flexing his muscles of independence, and Patrick was maintaining his authority in the home. The tension seemed to be growing worse, and they both felt like their backs were against the wall.

"Get out of my face. You're not my dad, and I'm sick of you trying to act like you are. How I treat my mom is none of your business!" Jimmy raised his voice as a red flush crept across his face.

"I'm the man of this house, and as long as you live here, you'll follow my rules whether you like it or not!" Patrick poked Jimmy in the chest as he made his point emphatically.

Jimmy pushed Patrick away from him and yelled, "I don't have to put up with this!" He stormed out the door.

Patrick was breathing hard. He contemplated whether he would run after Jimmy, call the police, or just let him go.

> ## POINT TO PONDER
>
> At the center, heart, or eye in every conflict storm is a calm, peaceful place where conflict is transformed and transcended and where learning, dialogue, and insight take place.
>
> **KENNETH CLOKE**

"Good morning, Joan. Have a seat." Stan stood and motioned Joan to a chair on the other side of his desk. "How's life been treating you lately?" he asked as they both sat down.

"Just fine," Joan responded tentatively. She knew she'd been asked into the captain's office for a reason, and she sensed the "sandwich method" of discipline unfolding.

"Joan, the reason I asked to see you is because I need to discuss a matter with you. It's been brought to my attention that you played a practical joke on a firefighter here in the station. My understanding is that someone could have been hurt. I want to give you the opportunity to tell your side of the story."

Joan cleared her throat and began. "Well, it really wasn't that big of a deal. I rigged Brad's locker. I thought he had a sense of humor. I guess I was wrong. My intention wasn't to physically harm him. It was just to play a little joke on him for all the wisecracks he makes."

"Let me make sure I understand. You initiated the practical joke, is that correct?" Stan paused to give her time to respond.

"Yes, but it wasn't a big deal, and he's been making wisecracks for way too long!" Joan was getting defensive.

"Right now, we're just dealing with the situation with you, Joan. I'll address the wisecracks with Brad later. Do you recall a meeting we had three months ago where we discussed the rules and regulations in regards to practical jokes? In that conversation do you remember the standard we agreed on?"

"I remember we had a meeting about harassment and stuff like that, but I wasn't harassing Brad." Joan crossed her arms over her chest and leaned back in her chair.

"I have the notes here in your file from our last meeting, and it clearly defines what we discussed. Please read over those notes before we continue." Stan slid the folder across the desk. Joan leaned forward and read through the file.

"I just can't see how a stupid little joke can be considered harassment." Joan didn't want to admit she was wrong.

"Joan, the last time we met, we specifically discussed practical jokes in the station and why they need to be avoided. This is the second complaint I've received, and as you can see from our notes, we discussed what the ramifications would be. At this point, I'm going to have to proceed with a written reprimand for your file." Stan paused and allowed Joan the opportunity to let it sink in.

"I get it, Stan. I really didn't think it was a big deal. I won't let it happen again. It's obvious that not everyone has a sense of humor around here."

"Joan, please understand that you are one of the best firefighters we have. You are valued in this department. We have to follow the regulations to reduce misunderstandings, conflicts, and accidents. I'm sure your intent wasn't malicious, but, nonetheless, we still have to follow the rules." Stan smiled, hoping to relieve some of the tension.

"I know." Joan sighed. "I guess I just don't like all the rules and regs, but I understand why they exist. I'll keep my practical jokes at home."

Stan stood up and shook Joan's hand. "Thank you, Joan, for making an effort to understand and work within department guidelines. You're a valuable asset here."

Joan shrugged her shoulders, forced a smile, and left his office.

"Look, Ben," Pamela said to her supervisor, "I'm already putting in more hours than I should be in my management position. When I was hired, I agreed to work thirty hours a week. I have two kids, and I have to pay for daycare. Besides, I don't want to be away from home any more than I already am. I realize there are deadlines that need to be met, but we are just too short staffed right now. Not only am I functioning as a manager, but I'm also doing projects that should be done by team members. We just don't have enough team members to do all of the projects we're asked to do." Pamela was making her case as calmly as possible.

Ben sat for a moment in silence. He nodded his head in empathetic understanding. "I realize how strained it is for everyone right now, Pam. I'm feeling the pressure myself. Unfortunately, the company isn't in a position to hire additional staff right now. The slow economy is taking its toll on earnings, and I'm being pressured to try to cut back as much as I can in every department. I'm trying to do that without losing staff and without losing production. That's a real challenge."

"I'm sure it is." Pam was trying to contain her frustration with the current level of stress in her department. "I don't know what else you expect me to do."

"Well, our customers expect the deadlines to be met, and we can't bring on extra staff. We need to find a way to increase production without additional staff. It will benefit everyone if we can."

Pam knew increased production meant more income for everyone in her department. Bonus commissions were paid based on productivity, and the faster they could produce results, the more they would benefit. She also knew that everyone in the department was spread too thin as it was. She knew there were many people in her department who didn't work full-time and had to pay for daycare services. She proposed a solution.

"Ben, I have an idea that I think would work for everyone. What if we allowed some of our staff members to take a few of these projects home and work on them from a 'virtual' office? Nearly everyone has computers at home with internet access. They could access our system and complete some of the projects from home. This would allow them to commit to more hours when needed without having to incur daycare expenses or experience the grief of spending too much time away from their families."

Ben thought for a moment. "You know, that's not a bad idea. We could establish a set number of hours that must be fulfilled here at the office, and then create a flexible schedule for the virtual office. As long as the deadlines are met and production is increased, there's no reason why we couldn't validate this option. Why don't you put together a formal proposal, and I'll work on some ideas too. Let's meet back in my office next Friday."

Pamela left the office with a sense of excitement and accomplishment. She knew this program could be a win–win for everyone if it was put together right. She was beginning to see light at the end of the tunnel.

Conflict In Relationship

In each of the three scenarios, we saw different approaches to resolving conflict used. The person using each approach may not have been aware of what he or she was doing, but the specific approaches were still used. The three general approaches are power, rights, and reconciliation.

Power—Who Is More Powerful?

This approach to resolving conflict involves the possibility of acts of aggression. Those who have the power can withhold benefits. Neither party is quite sure how far the other party will take the attack or the withdrawal.

Rights—Who Is Right and by What Standard?

This approach relies on agreed-upon rules, contracts, or minutes. Decisions are determined on precedent, equality, and seniority. Rights also need power to enforce rules and regulations.

Reconciliation of Interests

This approach takes into consideration the needs, values, and concerns of the individuals involved. It also addresses the fears and desires of both parties. This method relies on two important concepts:

- For every interest involved, there usually exists several possible positions that could satisfy it. Respect for everyone's participation and suggestions is a key factor.

- Behind opposed positions lie many more compatible interests than conflicting ones. It is important to look for commonalities, interests, and solutions. The focus should be on future shared benefits for both parties.

In the first example of the stepfather and son, Patrick used the

"Power" approach with Jimmy. As the conflict escalated, Patrick used aggression and force. The aggression isn't always physical. Sometimes it's verbal or manipulative power plays. The use of power is a very common strategy as people attempt to establish their position in personal and professional settings. (The next chapter will address the use of power more specifically.)

In the second example, Stan was using the "Rights" approach to resolving conflict with Joan. He was counting on the written rules and regulations of the organization to solve the problem. He referenced past notes that Joan couldn't argue with. He established that a virtual contract existed and needed to be adhered to in order to alleviate conflict.

In the last example, Pamela employed the "Reconciliation of Interests" approach, which Ben bought into immediately. The stress and conflict in the organization had been mounting, and there were two sides to the conflict. Pamela and Ben were able to brainstorm a possible solution that would bring the interest of both parties together. They sought commonalities and solutions instead of focusing on the differences in their needs.

There are times when you may see one or more of these approaches used in a conflict situation. You may have people who use the rights approach. When that approach fails, they may try the power approach. You may also find a group of individuals who are using the power approach and eventually come to the reconciliation of interests approach after much discussion.

At the heart of every conflict resolution is compromise. The Conflict Matrix depicts this concept. Look at the chart carefully.

When assertiveness and concern for self is high and concern for others and acceptance is low, "Force" will tend to be employed in conflict. In this case, people tend to force their ideas and opinions on others while dismissing their needs.

When assertiveness and concern for self is low and concern and acceptance for others is low, "Avoidance" will tend to be employed in conflict. In this case, people tend to withdraw and avoid the conflict, not caring either way.

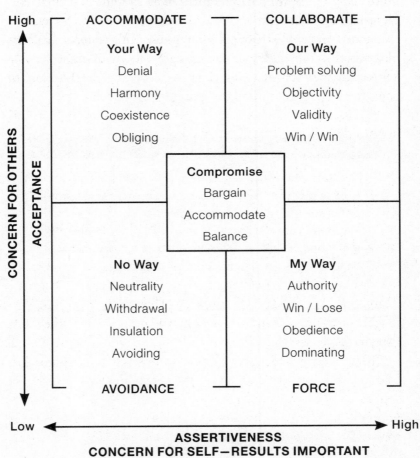

CONFLICT MATRIX

	ACCOMMODATE	COLLABORATE
High	**Your Way**	**Our Way**
	Denial	Problem solving
	Harmony	Objectivity
	Coexistence	Validity
	Obliging	Win / Win

Compromise
Bargain
Accommodate
Balance

	No Way	**My Way**
	Neutrality	Authority
	Withdrawal	Win / Lose
	Insulation	Obedience
	Avoiding	Dominating
	AVOIDANCE	FORCE

CONCERN FOR OTHERS / ACCEPTANCE (vertical axis, High to Low)

Low ← **ASSERTIVENESS** → High
CONCERN FOR SELF—RESULTS IMPORTANT

When assertiveness and concern for self is low and concern and acceptance for others is high, "Your Way" will tend to be employed in conflict. People accommodate others through obligation and coexistence, but they stuff their own needs.

When assertiveness and concern for self is high and concern and acceptance for others is high, "Our Way" will tend to be employed in conflict. In this case, people attempt to create a win/win situation through objective problem solving. They take into consideration the needs and interests of each other in an effort to come to the best conflict resolution possible.

At the heart of the matrix is compromise. This requires a balance of accommodating others while creating a win/win solution. No one has to force their way on to someone else. People bargain positions to come to a place of compromise where everyone can win.

POINT TO PONDER

The first agreements we reach are generally about ground rules or process. We do this because it is easier to agree on how people will talk to each other than on what they will say, they make everyone responsible for process improvement, and we can arrange the process so as to allow a deeper, more constructive content to emerge.

KENNETH CLOKE

8

The Influence of Power in Conflict

When two elephants fight, it is the
grass underneath that suffers.

T here is usually some form of power struggle in conflict situations. Power issues can be subtle and underground or they can be overt and straightforward. There are many catchphrases that describe the concept of power in human interaction. "There is a real power play going on in our organization." "She is a high-powered person." "He is a control freak." "She is the power behind the throne." "He is just being bullheaded." "My supervisor likes to throw her authority around." "That group just bulldozed over us." "I don't appreciate their strong-arm tactics."

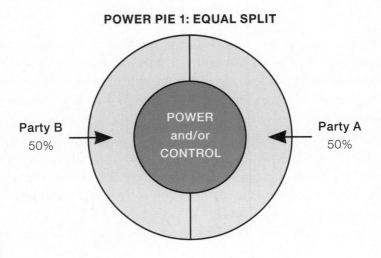

POWER PIE 1: EQUAL SPLIT

Party B
50%

POWER
and/or
CONTROL

Party A
50%

Your position in a conflict situation will often determine the outcome. Look at the two "Power Pies." The central factors in most conflicts involve power and control. In the first graph, party A has 50 percent of the power and/or control, and party B has 50 percent. In this situation, both parties have pretty equal footing.

In the second graph, party A has 70 percent of the power and/or control and party B has 30 percent. In this case, party B stands a pretty low chance of determining or dictating the outcome of the conflict.

POWER PIE 2: UNEQUAL SPLIT

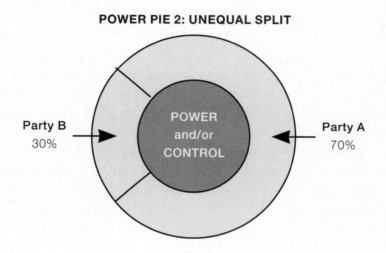

Sometimes the power pie can be very unbalanced. Some people use their positions of power and authority to cut the power pie nearly 100 percent in their favor. For example, a supervisor in an organization may use the position of authority and power to control conflict outcome. If someone approaches this person with a potential conflict, the supervisor may merely remind that person who is in charge of the largest piece of the power pie. "I'm your supervisor, so this is how it's going to be. If you don't like it, I suggest you find somewhere else to work." (Usually it will be much more subtle.) In this case, the power pie might be cut 99 percent to 1 percent.

In other situations, people may use their positions to positively influence others and empower others to maintain a positive level of control. In spite of their positions of authority, they may cut the power pie more evenly and respond differently. "Let's sit down and talk about some viable solutions to this conflict."

In some cases, a disproportionate power pie is absolutely necessary in conflict. For example, if you're a parent and you have a three-year-old who is challenging your authority and is ready to run into the street, you don't have time to argue about who's in control. You'll cut that power pie 100 percent in your favor and take complete control of that situation. Your position of authority and power will determine the outcome of the conflict.

In organizations, you're not dealing with three-year-olds (though it may seem like it at times), and you're not the parent (though it may seem like that too). Whether you deal with business relationships or personal ones, you'll encounter many different power approaches used by people throughout the course of their interactions with others. Here are some of the more common uses of power.

Positional power. Power can be seen when people are referring to their position. "Now hear this. I'm the father/mother." "I'm the boss." "I'm the teacher." "I'm the government official." "I'm somebody." "I'm in charge."

Expertise power. Power can be seen when individuals refer to their expertise. "I've got a college education." "I've been trained in this." "I've read books on this subject." "I've handled many of these situations before."

Seniority power. Power can be seen when people refer to their seniority. "I've been doing this job for fifteen years." "I've paid my dues." "I've been asked to consult in this area." "I've been promoted to senior team leader." "I didn't fall off the turnip truck last week."

Resource power. Power can be seen when the person is in control of resources. "I control the purse strings." "I write the checks in this organization." "I can cut off their supply any time I want."

Affiliation power. Power can be seen in networking contacts. "I know the boss." "I know who is in charge." "I have a friend who can pull strings." "I've got a guy who can get us a good deal." "I met the president the other day at lunch."

Personality power. Power can be seen in personality. "I just got elected to be class president." "They invited me to be master of ceremony." "I was on television last week." "I gave a speech at the club yesterday."

Godfathering power. Power can be seen in "godfathering." "Think of all the things I've done for you." "You're fortunate I was able to get you that job." "Don't worry about paying back that loan right away." "You owe me some respect. Remember, I recommended you for the position." The person being helped can become dependent or obligated to the helper. Helping others can be a masked high-power move.

Acting-out power. Power can be seen in the display and use of dysfunctional behavior. This can be in the form of yelling, crying, or rebellious actions. They are strong displays of emotion. People use this "acting out" to keep others from challenging their position or influence. Everyone becomes afraid of their strange or unpredictable behavior. The tendency is to back off and let them have their way.

Group pressure power. Power can be seen in using group pressure. The exercise of the "majority rules" or being "democratic" can force the people in disagreement into conformity and silence. This method can railroad decisions through board or committee meetings. It is especially effective if the confronting individual isn't present at the meeting. The person lobbying for his or her position can convince the group of a particular plan or decision. Then later, the person who is in disagreement is informed that the group had made a decision. How does the person argue against "the group"? This is a subversive technique for utilizing power and control.

Intimacy power. Power can be seen in intimacy. "We really have a close relationship." "I just got the latest word about that merger." "I can't believe you would treat me that way." "We've been friends for so many years."

Intimidation power. Power can be seen in intimidation. "Your job may be on the line over this issue." "If you can't get this job accomplished in time, you may not get the promotion." "I think your supervisor may need to know about this."

Silence power. Power can be seen in silence. There are not a lot of actual comments in silence. It's withholding information. It's keeping people "out of the loop" or in the dark. It can manifest by ignoring or not responding to written or verbal questions. It might show itself by excessive periods of noncommunication. And then when some communication does take place, the person exercising the silence pretends like nothing is wrong and everything is normal.

Silence can hide in a busy work schedule. It helps evade contact with the other party. Comments about being overloaded are provided as the excuse. There is mention of conflicts in time and an inability to get together. "I'm really sorry we haven't been able to touch base. My workload has been so heavy, you know." These are often followed by suggestions and promises of getting together soon.

Silence can even continue when the parties get together at home, work, or in social settings. Only small talk is allowed. Nothing of importance is shared. No issues are introduced or resolved. It is basically a shutting off of relationships. Silence is basically treating the other individual as a nonperson, as someone who doesn't exist. The Amish use shunning to control the behavior of those who might "walk to the beat of a different drummer" or who disagree with the leadership.

Communication silence is the most destructive force in relationships. It's quite common and used effectively at home, business, and in the community. It's often used to force individuals into submission or frustrate them without having to personally confront them. It's one of the most powerful forms of passive aggressiveness. It can also be used as a form of revenge and a method to hurt someone without "coming out into the open." No one will be able to directly accuse people using this technique because there no spoken comments or obvious nonverbal cues. The power person may even smile and pretend to be interested while using this subtle and powerful form of control. It's been said that "silence is full of words we never utter."

Privilege power. Power can be seen in withholding privileges. It may be found in the changing of a person's job to a lesser position of influence or responsibility. It can be used to deliberately frustrate people to the point where they get angry and quit or pull out of an intimate relationship. When that happens, the person withholding the privileges gets off scot-free because he or she wasn't the one who left. It was the other person, who could have stayed.

Passive-aggressive power. This behavior uses techniques like *chronic forgetfulness.* "Oh, I'm sorry. I simply forgot." Isn't it strange how we never forget the things we really want to do? Some common passive-aggressive behaviors include:

- *Chronic lateness:* Of *course*, there are lots of excuses, and they all sound good.

- *Chronic illness:* Promises have been made but the person doesn't want to keep them.

- *Conflicts in scheduling:* "Oh, I forgot. I scheduled two things at once." Isn't it interesting how your appointment is the one canceled?

- *Slips of speech:* Unkind words are said and then apologized for them. It seems accidental…at first, but it isn't long before a pattern emerges.

- *Unkind humor:* "Is that your face or did your neck throw up?" "Is that your head or did your body blow a bubble?" "Just kidding, you know." This is the double whammy. You get chopped by the joke and then by the follow-up comment that you have no sense of humor.

- *Evading issues and people:* This often inconveniences those who are evaded. Decisions are delayed and communication is stymied.

- *Acting out with nonverbal behavior:* Slamming doors, dropping things loudly, banging objects. When confronted, the person denies there is anything wrong.

The way you use power can leave a legacy that negatively affects relationships. It can create the desire to get even. Passive-aggressive behavior (as well as other negative uses of power) needs to be confronted. Confrontation can be a painful and difficult process. It can also be a freeing and healing process for both parties if approached properly and resolved.

When Abuse of Power Becomes Physical

Hopefully you'll never have to deal with the physical side of conflict and confrontation. As a rule of thumb, when people escalate conflict to the point of physical involvement, they have come to the end of their verbal skills. When they feel they can no longer communicate or get their point across, they lash out physically. They use and abuse physical power to get their way.

Physical conflict is an attempt to control the situation. Striking out can be an attempt to gain submission. It's a physical way to let the other person know who the boss is, who has the power, and who is in control. A physical display can also be an attempt to get the other party to back off or withdraw. It's not so much an attack as it is a protection device. Regardless of motivation, physical violence tends to separate people and escalate conflict.

Avoiding physical confrontation is obviously a safety issue for everyone involved and those close to the people involved. You can enhance your knowledge and sharpen your skills in verbally dealing with difficult people in your life. There are signs or "red flags" that wave before verbal conflict turns into physical conflict. It's important that you recognize them so you won't contribute to the stress of the situation. Do you notice these characteristics in the other person?

- tone of voice gets stronger
- volume of speech gets louder
- speed of speech increases
- name calling and swearing may be present
- warnings and threats are issued
- eyes focus and squint
- arms wave
- fists clench
- pacing ensues

- body language looks threatening
- objects might be thrown
- hitting of doors, walls, and other items start
- forward movement and space between people narrow
- territorial space is invaded

Hello. I think there's a message here. This is not brain surgery. This is not astrophysics. You are about to be assaulted. Be alert to these warning signals! When you see the winds of trouble coming, don't add extra energy to the tornado in front of you. The result may be devastating. Remember, most of the violence and even murders occur between people who know each other.

- Don't raise your voice.

- Remain calm and cool.

- Don't make fun of the person.

- Don't call him or her names.

- Don't accuse him or her.

- Don't make warnings and threats back.

- Don't taunt or belittle. Don't egg the person on. I strongly suggest you don't say, "Come on. Why don't you hit me?" I've counseled families where this was done. When the attack occurs, the person who was taunting can then stand back and say, "All I was doing was just talking, and then bam!" Then the person assaulted tries to convince everyone that she (or he) was the totally innocent victim. This becomes her excuse for getting out of the marriage. It helps the "victim" look better for the other person to be blamed.

- Physically remove yourself from the situation. Walk away—run if necessary. Do everything in your power to deescalate the situation. When all else fails say, "I need to go to the bathroom."

"Absolute power corrupts absolutely." You've heard that adage, I'm sure. Those who exercise negative power develop a false sense of worth. They believe their own press reports. They begin to design methods and systems to protect the power they have. They look down on those who have less power. It's also true that absolute powerlessness also corrupts. It forces people into positions where they have nothing to lose, so they fight back with rebellious intensity. Tyranny in any form creates and fosters revolution. Revolution can take various forms from extreme aggressiveness to passiveness.

When Great Britain ruled India, it was by sheer force. The Indian people were under subjection. Mahatma Gandhi challenged the might of the English using nonviolent resistance. He didn't have the wealth, unlimited resources, or the desire to use military strength. He depended on his strength of character. In the end, who was stronger? A wise grasshopper once said, "He who decides who has the power, has the power."

POINT TO PONDER

There is, of course, a fundamental distinction between power *against*, which instills fear; power *over*, which triggers resentment; power *for*, which encourages participation; and power *with*, which builds collaboration and trust.

KENNETH CLOKE

9

The Positive Power of Confrontation

Face the conflict. To run from it will be a continual race.

R.E. PHILLIPS

Denny's practical jokes are getting out of control. Will you talk to him about it?" Darlene was expressing her displeasure to Denny's direct supervisor, Cindy.

Cindy leaned forward and looked Darlene in the eye. "Have you talked to Denny about it yet?"

"No, and I really don't want to confront him on this. You're his boss, so I thought it would be better coming from you." Darlene avoided Cindy's intense stare.

After a long pause, Cindy took a deep breath and said, "Darlene, confrontation is not a bad thing. It will establish the boundaries you'd like to see in your working relationship with Denny. Not everyone feels the way you do, so Denny might not be aware that he's offending you. If you confront Denny with honesty, integrity, and respect, I'm sure he'll respond to your concern. If you confront him with the issue, and he fails to respond properly, I will be happy to talk with him."

Darlene leaned back in her chair and crossed her arms. "I don't want to make the working environment any more uncomfortable than it is. I don't want him to make my life miserable if I confront him and it makes him mad."

"The tension will only increase if you don't confront the situation. It won't go away on its own. Additionally, Denny is less likely to be resentful if you confront him first versus going over his head. If you confront him and he attempts to make your life miserable, you can be assured that I will intervene." Cindy smiled.

Darlene stared out the window. "Well, I guess it's worth a try. I'll talk to him today and let you know how it goes."

Not every person looks forward to dealing with confrontation. Some people's social style includes viewing confrontation negatively. In some cases, they've had very negative experiences with confronting others, so they give up. In other cases, they simply don't want to face the potential tension that might come with a confrontation.

POINT TO PONDER

Most people who are stuck in conflict have never met with their opponents or had an open, honest discussion— even of the superficial issues in their dispute, let alone the deeper issues that are keeping them at an impasse. When we ask people why they have not communicated important information about the deeper levels of their conflict to their opponents, they often say it is because their opponent is unwilling to listen, would not be interested in the information, or is untrustworthy. We then ask how they can know their opponent will not listen or is uninterested or untrustworthy if they are unwilling to speak.

KENNETH CLOKE

While initially it may seem difficult to confront conflict, confrontation actually reduces the amount of conflict you will face. The following chart depicts the amount of success in reducing conflict relative to the conflict intensity. If the conflict intensity is extremely low, you have concealed conflict in your life (unexpressed). Coupled with the low conflict intensity is the low productiveness of reducing the actual conflict. If the conflict intensity is high and you have unrestrained

HOW DO YOU DEAL WITH CONFLICT?

Compromise
Walk around
the problem

Withdraw
Walk away

Confront
Blast through;
deal with it

Deny
Ignore

expression of conflict, you will experience the same problem—the productiveness of reducing the conflict will suffer.

Once you strike a balance with managed conflict, you'll begin to confront the conflicts in your life in a positive manner. The conflict is being confronted (or expressed) in a balanced manner, and as a result, the productiveness of the confliction reduction will be successful.

POINT TO PONDER

We need to recognize that every conflict contains hidden lessons that fuel our growth, change, learning, awareness, intimacy, effectiveness, and successful relationships. We should not be frightened of moving toward their center.

KENNETH CLOKE

DEGREE OF SUCCESS IN CONFLICT REDUCTION

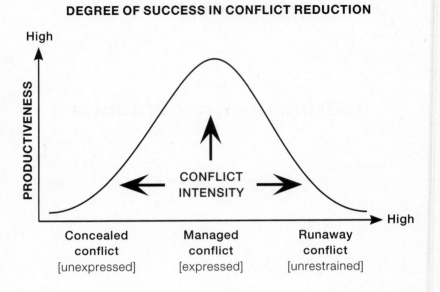

THE MONSTER OF CONFLICT

I was minding myself when the monster appeared.
He was ten steps behind me, and gaining, I feared.
I thought if I shunned him, he might disappear,
But luck would not have it—his steps only neared.
I rounded the corner and closer he came,
Atrocious and frightening, shouting my name.
I thought if I shunned him, he might do the same,
But his shadow was growing; he would not be tamed.
I stopped in my steps and turned swift around.
I confronted the monster, and he made not a sound.
He crumbled and shriveled and fell to the ground,
Then his crumbs blew away, and not a piece could be found.

KIMBERLY ALYN

10

Making the Confrontation

*Tyranny, like hell, is not easily conquered; yet we
have this consolation with us, that the harder
the conflict the more glorious the triumph.*

THOMAS PAINE

Approaching conflict is a very delicate process. While confrontation is positive and healthy if done correctly, it can be detrimental if done poorly. Careful consideration should be made when confronting another person on a conflict issue. If your tendency is to avoid a confrontation, try to resist that. Step out of your comfort zone to confront the conflicts in your life. If your tendency is to confront conflict head-on without much consideration of the process, resist this tendency and think through some of the important factors before confronting.

Pick the Right Plan

There is no single, perfect plan for every conflict situation you'll encounter. There are, however, principles that will assist you in confrontation and conflict resolution. Your desire is to seek out the most effective principles and apply them to your situation. It may require a mixing, matching, and combination of approaches. This book is designed to give you those tools. It's important to understand social styles and how everyone is unique in approaching conflict. Methods of conflict reduction, studies of body language, and listening skills can be combined to make conflict resolution more productive.

Understanding Social Styles

The term "social styles" refers to a person's natural inclinations inherited from his or her parents. This is sometimes referred to as "temperament." "Personality" is a little different. That's how a person expresses his or her inherited social style. "Character" is the quality of the individual's personality and can be affected by morals, values, and ethics.

The social style concept focuses on actual displayed behaviors rather than motivations behind behavior. Most of us judge ourselves by our intentions; however, when it comes to others, we judge by words and deeds. When we disagree with someone else's words and behavior or they disagree with ours, conflict arises.

Social style research indicates there are four basic types: Analyticals, Drivers, Amiables, and Expressives. The following charts offer quick overviews of what the four social styles find valuable and what they find annoying.

ANALYTICALS	
WHAT THEY VALUE	**WHAT ANNOYS THEM**
Security	Inaccuracy
Accuracy	Incompetence
Stability	Change
Rules and regulations	Aggressiveness
Quality	Shouting
Structure	Evasiveness
Efficiency	Mediocrity
Facts	Inadequacy
Competence	Exaggeration
Details	Invasiveness
Tradition	Clutter
Critical thinking	Disorganization
Organization	Clamor
Logic	Hastiness

DRIVERS	
WHAT THEY VALUE	**WHAT ANNOYS THEM**
Achievement	Indecisiveness
Challenge	Boredom
Success	Small talk
Power	Details
Speed	Hypersensitivity
Control	Overemotional
Responsibility	Dependency
Goals	Excuses
Debates	Irresponsibility
Competition	Lethargy
Leadership	Laziness
Independence	Procrastination
Decisiveness	Taking orders
Productivity	Overanalyzing

AMIABLES	
WHAT THEY VALUE	**WHAT ANNOYS THEM**
Contribution	Conflict
Comfort	Impatience
Compassion	Disrespect
Cooperation	Discourteousness
Friendliness	Insensitivity
Peacefulness	Harshness
Loyalty	Rushing
Approval	Pressure
Cohesiveness	Tension
Trust	Controversy
Kindness	Disharmony
Relationships	Yelling
Benevolence	Pushiness
Coaching	Rudeness

EXPRESSIVES	
WHAT THEY VALUE	WHAT ANNOYS THEM
Freedom	Rules
Excitement	Structure
Adventure	Schedules
Flexibility	Routine
Spontaneity	Tedium
Vision	Stagnation
Enthusiasm	Slowness
Change	Boredom
Unpredictability	Ritual
Uniqueness	Unoriginality
Creativity	Lack of creativity
Innovation	Details
Versatility	Formality

GENERAL OVERVIEW OF THE FOUR SOCIAL STYLES				
Areas	ANALYTI-CALS	DRIVERS	AMIABLES	EXPRESSIVES
Reaction	Slow	Swift	Unhurried	Rapid
Orientation	Thinking and fact	Action and goal	Relationship and peace	Involvement and intuition
Likes	Organization	To be in charge	Close relationships	Much interaction
Dislikes	Involvement	Inaction	Conflict	To be alone
Maximum effort	To organize	To control	To relate	To involve
Minimum concern	For relationships	For caution in relationships	For affecting change	For routine
Behavior directed toward achievement	Works carefully and alone— *primary effort*	Works quickly and alone— *primary effort*	Works slowly and with others— *secondary effort*	Works quickly and with team— *secondary effort*

Behavior directed toward acceptance	Impresses others with precision and knowledge— *secondary*	Impresses others with individual effort— *secondary*	Gets along as integral member of group— *primary*	Gets along as exciting member of group— *primary*
Actions	Cautious	Decisive	Slow	Impulsive
Skills	Good problem-solving skills	Good administrative skills	Good counseling skills	Good persuasive skills
Decision-making	Avoids risks, based on facts	Takes risks, based on intuition	Avoids risks, based on opinion	Takes risks, based on hunches
Use of time	Slow, deliberate, disciplined	Swift, efficient, impatient	Slow, calm, undisciplined	Rapid, quick, undisciplined*

Each social style has a general response to conflict. Analyticals will withdraw in an attempt to save face and think through the problem. They avoid and dodge undesirable situations and are annoyed by people who come on too strong.

Drivers attempt to control the person or situation. They tend to impose their thoughts and opinion on others in the midst of conflict. If they feel they are losing control, they tend to over-control to compensate. They are very strong-willed and can be demanding in conflict.

Amiables will give in to avoid confrontation. They don't feel conflict is worth it. They would rather save the relationship, even if it hurts them. Amiables appear to be in agreement on the outside, but they may be resentful on the inside.

Expressives will attack in the midst of conflict. They may use condemnations and put-downs to discredit others. They have very strong emotions and feelings, and they'll let others know exactly what they think. Expressives can chew others out, and they have a tendency to raise their voices when conflict escalates.

---

* Merrill and Reid, *Personal Styles and Effective Performance (CRC Press, 1981), as noted in* Bolton and Bolton, "Social Style/Management Style" (Amacom, 1984).

This chart shows the four usual responses to conflict by social style.

RESPONSES TO CONFLICT BY SOCIAL STYLE	
Analyticals — Withdraw They tend to become less assertive, more controlled, hold in feelings, don't share ideas. Basically they avoid, dodge, escape, and retreat from other people and/or undesirable situations.	**Drivers — Dominate** They tend to become over-assertive, unbending, over-controlling, and demanding. Strong-willed, they attempt to impose their thoughts and feelings on others.
Amiables — Give In They tend to give in to keep the peace and reduce conflict. They appear to agree with others when inside they disagree. They strongly desire to save the relationship even if it hurts themselves.	**Expressives — Attack** They tend to emotionally attack others and their ideas, using condemnations and put-downs. Expressives have strong emotions and reveal how they feel about things.

Responding to Each Social Style During Conflict

As you can see, each social style responds differently to conflict, especially when they feel like their backs are against the wall. You'll have your own unique response as well, which may escalate the conflict. Learning to respond to each social style's general responses in conflict will help reduce tension and go a long way toward resolving the problem.

Responding to the "Withdrawing Analytical"

As observed earlier, Analyticals tend to withdraw from conflict to save face. They want to deal with the problem alone, with a minimum amount of interaction with others. They need time to think about the problem, situation, or relationship. They need as much information as possible in order to deal effectively with their distress.

Don't keep pushing Analyticals for a response or insist on their increased participation before they have adequate time to think. They need time and space, so give it to them. Since Analyticals are by nature systematic, make sure you approach their problem with a step-by-step solution. Help them set up a plan to gather more problem-solving data to consider. Ask them for a special time to discuss the matter after they've had time to think it through.

If you're an Expressive or a Driver, your natural tendency is to tell not ask. If you want to reduce conflict with an Analytical, practice patience. Speak softer, slower, and ask questions. "What ideas do you have for a solution?" "How do you feel about doing A, B, and C?" When you approach them with a step-by-step solution for review, you are talking their language.

Responding to the "Dominating Driver"

Drivers feel like they have lost control in conflict situations, leaving them with no personal choices. The tension they feel drives them to get something accomplished, and they may attempt to regain control by over-controlling.

Don't try to compete with Drivers or match force with force because competition is their specialty. Don't argue or debate with them. They can verbally shred you to pieces in a matter of seconds. Don't back down from them either, even when they come on strong. Drivers respect people who hold their ground, even if that person disagrees with the position of the Driver. They just don't want you attempting to persuade them to abandon their own position.

When in the midst of conflict with Drivers, don't inundate them with too much detail or take too long to get to the point. They will get very irritated and cut you off to get something accomplished. Try to redirect the strong energies of the Driver toward positive goals, achievements, and actions that you can support. Drivers appreciate goals and the freedom to choose their own methods of reaching those goals. Help them decide on a goal and a path for reaching that goal. Attempting to control Drivers will cause more conflict and cause them to over-control.

Responding to the "Give In" Amiable

Amiables will always appear to be in agreement during a conflict. They'll try to maintain relationships at all costs, even personal hurt. A gentleman approached me after a seminar and said, "I realize now that my wife was an Amiable. We never really fought because as soon as we would get into conflict, she would always agree with me. It always seemed like everything was fine. She saw things my way, and we got along great. So I thought. After eleven years, I came home one day and all her stuff was packed and she was gone. She left a note saying she couldn't take it anymore. All along I thought we were doing just fine. But she was miserable and didn't want to rock the boat. I wish I knew then what I know now."

A sign of compliance and agreement by an Amiable is not a sign of commitment. They often have inner turmoil they don't want to share. They fear backlash or continued conflict if they share what they really think. Consequently, they simply agree with the person they're in conflict with and give in.

If you're in conflict with an Amiable, don't push them for a response. Amiables don't appreciate people who come on too strong. Don't express anger or raise your voice. Don't argue or insist on your way. This will only push them deeper into their pattern of acquiescence as they struggle to save the relationship. Instead, encourage them to share their feelings. Ask them for constructive criticism regarding the conflict. If they get the courage to tell you, don't make them sorry they did. Don't belittle them or negate their input or you may never get it again.

Amiables like to feel they're needed and can help others out. Tell them you would like to work on the conflict situation, but you need some concrete suggestions from them. Work side-by-side with them through the problem-solving steps they suggest. Establish some form of evaluation process. They'll respond cautiously, so move slowly and be patient.

Responding to the "Attacking Expressive"

Expressives become very selfish, emotional, and assertive when their backs are against the wall. They'll vent their feelings by attacking the situation and the people involved. They won't hesitate to tell you what they really think—and they'll do it with gusto.

Don't evaluate the emotional outburst of an Expressive. It won't help to intellectually defend yourself either. Don't let Expressives draw you into their tantrums. Don't try to out-shout an Expressive because you'll most likely lose. Listen sympathetically and accept their emotions without getting emotionally involved yourself.

Let them get their emotions out of their systems. If you block the venting of the Expressives, you may provoke an even greater explosion. Once they get their emotions off their chests, you can help them focus on creative alternatives for handling problems in the future. You might try something like, "Now that you've shared your feelings about it, how are we going to handle this problem the next time it comes up?" Expressives are creative individuals. Once they move out of the negative behaviors, they'll return to their positive dispositions.

For an easy-to-read, in-depth study of social styles, check out *How to Deal with Annoying People: What to Do When You Can't Avoid Them*, by Bob Phillips and Kimberly Alyn (Eugene, OR: Harvest House Publishers, 2011).

Pick the Right Motivation

Determine in your mind to take the principled approach to resolving conflict. Attempt to remain friends with anyone you face in a conflict situation. This may not be possible in every case, but it certainly should be the goal.

Determine in your mind to not strike back and get revenge. Making threats or demands will not bring resolution. It will only create more conflict. "Digging in" and becoming inflexible seldom solve anything and lead to separation.

Determine in your mind to be the "change agent" in the conflict situation. Don't wait for the other person to make the first move. You make it. Sitting around waiting for the other person to change equals no change at all. *You need to control your part in the conflict.* Face it, own it, and deal with it. Avoiding conflict and confrontation makes the situation worse. Families are disrupted, organizations suffer, and personal effectiveness is reduced. Positive confrontation is a sign of caring.

Determine in your mind to develop a thick skin. Don't take everything so personally. Relax. Ease up. Chill out a little. A little humor might be what is needed. Someone said, "We would worry less about what others think of us if we realized how seldom they do."

Determine in your mind to allow the other person to save face. Don't go for the throat. Public humiliation isn't necessary. There is no reason to place a scarlet "C" on their forehead to let everyone know they are a carrier of conflict. Grow up. Be mature. Be the bigger person.

Picking the Right Time

The following principles are helpful to keep in mind when considering the timing of a confrontation meeting.

Poor Timing

Poor timing...

- *rushes* the other party. It takes them off guard and doesn't give them time to think.
- *pushes* the other party to respond. It reduces their ability to respond in fairness, with full disclosure, and with openness.
- *catches* the other party when they may be emotionally weak, physically tired, encountering an illness, or when they are under time constraints.
- *forces* the other party to respond negatively, especially if the confrontation takes place in a public setting where embarrassment may occur or private information is made public.

Poor timing is initiated when a person wants to catch the other in a surprise attack. This verbal ambush can be a way to get revenge and cause hurt. It's selfish to blurt out grievances any time you feel like it. Wise King Solomon said, "Like apples of gold in settings of silver is a word spoken in right circumstances" (Proverbs 25:11 NASB).

Good Timing—The Sooner the Better

As a rule, it's not good to let too much time go by between the conflict and the confrontation. By dealing with the conflict immediately, you have the best opportunity to resolve it. As time goes on, good

UNDERSTANDING CONFLICT TIMING

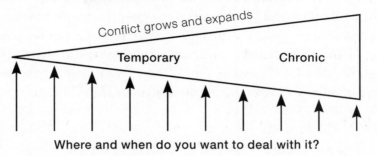

Conflict grows and expands

Temporary   Chronic

Where and when do you want to deal with it?

options for resolution begin to diminish. Dealing with the problem as soon as possible is best. First, it lets you deal with issues while they're fresh in your mind. Second, it helps to lessen the build-up of hurt or animosity that might be generated over a period of time. How long do you usually wait? What has been the pattern of how and when you face people you have conflicts with?

You might consider dealing with a conflict issue within four hours or up to twenty-four hours from the occurrence. This provides time to think through the situation and allows for unforeseen interruptions that might transpire. There might be circumstances that create a need for extending the time before the confrontation. However, the idea is to do it on the sooner side rather than the later side. The apostle Paul, speaking to husbands and wives who were encountering conflict, said, "Don't let the sun go down with you still angry—get over it quickly" (Ephesians 4:26).

When You're Feeling Good

Determine the best time for your schedule and the pressures you're facing. It's not good to go into a heavy discussion when you're not feeling good physically. It's better to approach the other party when you're rested and your stress level is low.

Set a Date

For some meetings, it's good to set a specific time and date. This helps you get organized in your thinking and get prepared in your presentation. It also helps to reduce the emotional component that will be present in your discussion. By having an agreed-on time, both parties involved will have an opportunity to think about the meeting beforehand.

There will be occasions when it won't be possible to set a specific date for the meeting. You may have to wait for the right moment and opportunity to approach the individual. In this case it's important to be prepared. You would be wise to map out or outline the items that need to be discussed. When the right moment comes, you'll be ready to share your thoughts and not be caught off guard.

Listen to Your Heart

Sometimes you may not be sure when it's the right time to talk with someone. What do you do in that case? Get organized with what you want to share. Have it well-rehearsed in your mind. Then relax. Wait patiently. The right moment will eventually come. You'll know it's the right moment when you find yourself alone with the person you need to talk to. Your heart will race a little faster and you'll ask yourself, *Is this the right time?* When you find that you can't hold back your thoughts and you have to speak, it will be the right time. Trust your gut.

"But what if the right time doesn't come?" you ask. Still trust your gut. When you find you must have the issue resolved, you may need to take the initiative. Go ahead. It will be all right. Remember, you have prepared for this meeting.

POINT TO PONDER

We all know that it takes time to resolve organizational disputes, yet it also takes time to not resolve them. If we count up the time and money we routinely spend on unresolved conflicts, it is nearly always far in excess of the time and money it would take to sit down and work out solutions.

KENNETH CLOKE

Pick the Right Place

The ideal location for confrontation is neutral territory. Remember, in most sports activities the home team has the advantage. The same is true in heavy or difficult discussions. Whoever's turf the confrontation takes place on has a slight advantage. Resolving the conflict will be easiest on neutral ground. A local restaurant is a good idea. Talking over issues in public often keeps emotions from rising to an unproductive level. Neutral ground might also be a park bench or going for a walk and talking. Discussing issues on a walk is very effective. Walking lets off a lot of nervous energy that might be present. It doesn't require continued eye contact, which is sometimes difficult. It also helps both parties focus on the decision of moving forward. It's almost like discussing a third-party issue that is in front of them. Many husbands and wives find that this is a positive and productive way to talk over disagreements.

I have a friend who had to meet with some very dissatisfied customers. They were upset about a procedure that had taken place which caused disruption in their company. He and his assistant met them in a room with a large, long table. They sat on one side of the table and the two unhappy customers sat on the other side. Then one of the unhappy men got up and went to a chalkboard. He picked up an eraser and walked to the far end of the table and set it down.

He returned to his seat and sat down. He pointed to the eraser and said, "You see, that's our problem. Let's talk about it." The use of the eraser to represent the issue or problem was an effective way to objectify the discussion and keep the discussion from becoming filled with personal attacks.

Some issues can't be discussed in public. They must be dealt with on strictly a private level. Some matters need eye-to-eye contact. And in a less-than-perfect world, we're not always able to choose neutral territory. In these cases, go ahead and make the best of the conversation regardless of where you happen to be.

What do you do if you're caught in a situation where it's the wrong time and the wrong place? Take a deep breath. Decide to be mature and controlled. Assess what the real issue is. Listen carefully to what is being said, and read the emotions behind it. Try not to take it too personally and lose perspective. And rise to the occasion with a respectful response.

A number of years ago, I was in a hotel lobby with a group of friends. One of the individuals in the group wasn't happy with what the group wanted to do. He'd made plans for the day for the entire group without asking them. When he shared his planned schedule with the group, they weren't excited about it. They wanted to take the day's activities in another direction.

At this point, the individual threw an adult temper tantrum in the hotel lobby. He raised his voice and made accusations. He put people down. He created a scene that drew the attention of everyone in the vicinity. We were all embarrassed and caught off guard. He made his final closing statement and was about to stomp off.

With a louder voice than usual, I said, "Oh no you don't! You don't create a public scene and just walk off. We're going to stay right here and finish this discussion." Everyone in the group turned and looked at me. You can well believe that everyone in the lobby was really interested now. The stage was definitely set for confrontation.

If this particular conflict would have been allowed to occur in public and not be addressed when it happened, the individual would have believed he could say anything and then just retreat. He would continue to use his manipulative "hit and run" behavior as a scare tactic. The mature thing was to confront the behavior that was unacceptable. In most situations, I prefer to talk with people in a private setting. However, we don't always have that luxury. You can mark it down as a general rule that if someone makes an issue public, you have to deal with the issue publicly.

POINT TO PONDER

Every conflict contains at least three paths:

1. One moving backward toward impasse, enmity, and adversarial relationships.
2. One moving forward toward resolution, respect, and collaborative relationships.

3. One moving deeper into the heart of the conflict toward evolution and learning, transformation and transcendence.

KENNETH CLOKE

Pick the Right Goal

In any attempt to resolve conflict, it's important to pick the right goal. How would you like to see the discussion end? What outcome would be best for all parties involved? What would be the ideal solution?

It's also important to enter the confrontation with a positive outcome in mind. Your attitude will play a significant part in the resolution encounter. If you enter the confrontation with the desire to hurt the other party, that will probably occur. If you desire to get revenge, you most likely will. If you want to let the other party know you're mad, you will succeed.

The best approach is to enter the confrontation with the desire to see positive change. You can be positive even if the other person is negative. You can help set the tone for mutual resolution. Remember, you will reap what you sow.

What changes would you like to see in the situation or between the people involved? Have you heard the adage, "If you aim at nothing, you'll hit it every time"? It's true. A fuzzy goal or objective will end in a fuzzy resolution.

In determining your goals, you first need to understand that everything might not work out the way you desire. You may have to make some adjustments in your thinking and develop alternatives or backup plans. You might consider making three lists. The first list is ideal resolution results you'd like to see. The second list focuses on the things you might not totally like but would accept. This could include things you'd be willing to give up and things you'd change for the other party. The third list is your bottom line. What things will you not give up? What things will you fight for? What things will put your back against the wall?

Once you've established some guidelines for your confrontation, you can take steps to resolve the conflict. The next factor to consider are the words you'll use when you initiate the confrontation. The next chapter provides some practical tools for choosing your words carefully.

POINT TO PONDER

In our experience, there are five widespread, chronic sources of workplace and organizational conflict:

1. A lack of clear and courageous leadership

2. A lack of agreement over values, vision, mission, and goals

3. A lack of clarity regarding roles and responsibilities

4. A lack of support for collaboration and participation in decision-making over issues that are important in people's lives

5. A lack of equality and fairness in the distribution of resources and pay

KENNETH CLOKE

11

Choose Your Words Carefully

*The tongue of the wise makes knowledge
acceptable, but the mouth of fools spouts folly.*

PROVERBS 15:2 NASB

Choosing your words carefully is one of the keys to successful conflict resolution. The words you use can create defensiveness or acceptance. Your words can cause someone to dismiss your message or accept it. Let's look at some valuable tools for approaching conflict.

"I Statements"

One of the keys to effective conflict resolution is to use "I statements" rather than "you statements." "I statements" are assertive and confrontive. "You statements" are aggressive and attacking. I statements let the other party know you have strong ideas and convictions. It gives them a gauge of how strongly you feel about a certain issue. Your strong beliefs and emotions can be shared without attacking the other person. You're simply letting the other person know how you think and feel about the conflict between the two of you. If you respond by saying, "You idiot," the war will probably be on.

The wonderful thing about I statements is that you can talk about both positive and negative thoughts and feelings. The use of I statements reduces the risk of the separation of parties over the conflict. You don't have to start out the conversation on a strong level. You can slowly and gently raise or lower the intensity as needed.

- "When you embarrassed me in the meeting, I felt *surprised* and *caught off guard.*"
- "When you embarrassed me in the meeting, I felt a little *annoyed.*"
- "When you embarrassed me in the meeting, I felt *irritated.*"
- "When you embarrassed me in the meeting, I felt *hurt* and *disgusted.*"
- "When you embarrassed me in the meeting, I felt very *angry.*"

I statements help you focus on behavior and reduce the probability of attacking the other party on a personal basis. The use of I statements helps you crystallize your thinking and organize your presentation of the issue. This clarity of thinking will assist you in keeping on track.

Another wonderful benefit from the use of I statements is that it helps to "bleed off" any tension you're feeling. This is especially important if the other party doesn't admit to any part in the conflict or refuses to consider changing his or her behavior.

POINT TO PONDER

It is especially difficult for us to be honest with those we dislike or who dislike us. This is because superficiality, silence, secrets, and lies seem less risky and more powerful to us than vulnerability, honesty, shared responsibility, and open communication. Aggression and self-defense give an appearance of honesty and are more readily accepted in organizational environments because they are instinctual, seemingly strong, grounded in distrust, and difficult to control.

KENNETH CLOKE

I statements give clarity, focus thinking, and reduce personal and group tension. The results often create more confidence in the individual initiating the confrontation. A platform is created for true communication to take place. Increased respect is generated in the confronted party because the confronter is being honest and straightforward in his or her presentation. This type of communication can help strengthen relationships and the bond between people.

I have a friend who had to confront his next-door neighbor over a very emotionally loaded situation. My friend's daughter came to him one day and related how the next-door neighbor had been touching her over her clothes in private areas of her body. She was around seven at the time.

Understandably, my friend was very angry and feeling protective. He shared with me the struggle he went through. He had strong winds of emotions blowing through him. He was a father. He was a minister. He was a man. He'd been trained in conflict resolution, yet it was hard to control his emotions in this most personal situation.

When he went next door to confront his neighbor regarding the matter, he knew he had to be in control of his thoughts and emotions. When his neighbor opened the door, my friend said, "I'm so mad at you, I could rip you to pieces." He later told me, "I had to use I statements. Even if I was extremely mad, I needed to let him know how I was feeling and how important the issue was to me. If I would have used You statements and attacked him personally, he might have responded with his own 'You' words. That would have most likely escalated the situation to an out-of-control level. At that point, the headlines the following day might have read, 'Enraged father kills next-door neighbor.'"

Using I statements will help you even in the most difficult situations.

POINT TO PONDER

Remember that even though someone pushes your button, it is still your button, and you always have a choice in how you respond.

KENNETH CLOKE

Focus on the Issue Not on the Person

A second key concept in communicating during conflict is to deal with or confront the issue, not the person. This requires sticking to the facts and the actual situation or behavior. It's important not to try to guess the motivation behind the behavior or action. When you deal with just the behavior and not the motivation, it opens the door for change. People tend to resent and get angry when their motivation is under attack. Even if you're correct in your evaluation, the other people's pride and desire to save face may keep them from responding in a positive manner. Keep in mind that effective confrontation involves telling the other people the effect their behavior has on *you*.

Avoid "Time Bomb" Words

A third key to positive conflict communication is to avoid "time bomb" words. These are words such as "always" and "never" that tend to blow the situation out of proportion. "You *always* forget to call home when you're going to be late." "*Every time* we get into a discussion, you get mad." "You *never* do anything right." "You're *forever* complaining." "You *constantly* interrupt me when I'm talking." "*Every moment* we're together is filled with arguments." "Can't you do *anything* right?" "Trying to talk to you is a *never-ending* struggle."

These types of cataclysmic statements broaden and escalate conflict. They sound extreme and accusatory to the listener's ear and blow up in the other people's minds and hinder progress. They sidetrack conversations down "rabbit trails." The listeners feel attacked, and the people defend themselves by responding to the hostility focused in their direction. Or the listeners might turn around and attack the person in retaliation. "I remember that I called you last Tuesday night and told you I would be late." "I wasn't mad when we talked about this at breakfast." "I cleaned up the garage like you asked me to." "I don't complain half as much as you do." "Talk about being interrupted. I can't even get a word in edgewise." "You're right, I can't do anything right. I didn't even marry the right person." "Well, if it's so much of a struggle, maybe we'd better part ways."

Be Specific

The fourth key in effective conflict communication is to be specific. Share the concrete and tangible effects the situation is having in your life. The purpose of this conversation is to resolve the conflict. You also want to get your needs met without the other people becoming and remaining defensive.

Each confrontation conversation isn't necessarily a time to send out all possible solutions. A change in a person's behavior and attitude doesn't always take place when confrontation occurs or when the first resolution point is reached. Sometimes it may take weeks or months.

Ideally, confrontation resolution is simply a defense of a person's rights in a nonjudgmental manner. Hopefully resolution will take place on the sooner side rather than on the later side.

POINT TO PONDER

When people go 'round and 'round the same arguments, it is because there is something fundamental, durable, and infinite at the center of the circle of their conflict waiting to be recognized and addressed. The closer people get to what lies at the center of their conflict, the more exhilarating, profound, and rewarding the conflicts become.

KENNETH CLOKE

Look at the following four-part confrontation message that's designed to assist you in forming your thoughts about the conflict situation. Hopefully, it will help you stay on track in your discussions with the people you have conflicts with. This matrix may be applied to problems at home, at work, or in your community.

When you... In the process of describing the undesired behavior, be sure to be accurate and specific. Keep the description of the behavior as brief as possible. Go right to

FOUR-PART CONFRONTATION MESSAGE

WHEN YOU...

In a nonjudgmental manner, describe the *conflicting* or *offending behavior* in specific and concrete terms.

I FEEL...

In a nonjudgmental manner, disclose *your feelings* about the conflicting or offending behavior.

BECAUSE...

In a nonjudgmental manner, state the *concrete* and *tangible effects* on you and your schedule.

I WOULD LIKE...

In a nonjudgmental manner, state the *specific* and *tangible behavior* you would like to see changed.

the point in crystal-clear terms. Be careful not to use "time bomb" words, such as "always," "never," and "every time."

I feel... The disclosure of feelings should accurately reflect the intensity of your emotion. If you're angry...own it using "I" words. If you're only a little irritated, don't exaggerate and make it sound worse than it is. Clearly state your irritation. Don't use words that make judgments or are designed to hurt the individual being confronted. An example of a judgment word is "disappointed." That word is often used to make the other person feel guilty or uncomfortable.

Because... In the process of sharing the tangible effects of the offending behavior, try not to turn it into a relationship problem. Keep the description of the effects *objective* rather than *subjective*. To help make the issue concrete, you may need to share how their behavior costs you money. Their actions may harm your possessions. Their deeds may cost you extra time or interfere with your work effectiveness. Their conduct may endanger your job or reputation.

I would like... The resolution of conflict is usually oriented toward the future. For this reason, it's important to state clearly the behavior you believe is acceptable. This gives the person a goal to work toward and an opportunity to change. Along with what you would like to see changed, it's good to share what you are willing to do to help the person be successful in implementing the resolution. When both parties work toward a shared future goal, hope is engendered and harmony and resolution are promoted.

In considering the delivery of your four-part message, it's good to ask yourself, "Do I have a right to confront?" This helps you filter out your motivation and hone in on your possible approach. There are different approaches for when you talk to a boss, a coworker, a friend, or a family member.

You might find it beneficial to write out your message. This will help you be specific and not wander. You also might be wise to ask yourself if confrontation is worth it. Could this be risky for this relationship or this job? Sometimes confrontation is necessary and must be done. Other times, it's good to have thick skin and strong shoulders to let some offenses run off. Wise King Solomon said, "A man's discretion makes him slow to anger, and it is his glory to overlook a transgression" (Proverbs 19:11 NASB).

You might find it helpful to role-play your message with a friend. Have your friend pretend to be the individual to be confronted. This practice will help you know what you want to say and how to say it. Your friend could give you helpful hints. He or she might suggest you leave out a particular thought or put it in a different way. If you don't feel comfortable sharing with a friend, you would do well to rehearse your confrontation in private.

Once you decide a confrontation must take place, don't put it off for long. That only makes the situation worse. Be sure to be consistent in your message. It must make sense. Don't add a host of unnecessary details. Extra details often confuse and sidetrack from the heart of the matter.

Expect the other person to become defensive. After your first presentation of the four-part message—the "When you... / I feel... /

Because… / I would like… —stop and let the person respond. Actively listen to what the person says. There may be tension between you. Don't run from it. When the tension lowers, return to your original message.

Even though confrontation may take place, it doesn't mean resolution has occurred. Resolution begins to take place when the other party buys into and owns their part of the problem. This buy-in must be followed by a *mutually agreed on solution* to the difficulty. There should also be a follow-up plan to confirm the effectiveness of the solution.

Unfortunately, not all confrontations are successful. When a confrontation has fallen on deaf ears, it might be time to go back to the drawing board. You might ask yourself, "Was I too judgmental? Was I not specific enough with the tangible effects on me? Did I send an inconsistent message? Did I pussyfoot around or sugarcoat the message and let the person off the responsibility hook? Did I get angry and say things I wish I hadn't? Did I make the problem worse by arguing?"

One of the most common responses to confrontation is defensiveness. In the next chapter, we'll look at some conflict avoidance techniques people tend to use when they become defensive. We'll also discover practical methods for keeping the confrontation resolution process moving in a positive direction.

POINT TO PONDER

Many conflicts involve intense emotions, negative behaviors, miscommunications, contrasting cultural norms, jumbled intentions, false expectations, inconsistent attitudes, and dysfunctional systems, any one of which can increase the level of chaos and complexity.

KENNETH CLOKE

12

Observing Body Language

*He alone is an acute observer, who can
observe minutely without being observed.*

JOHANN KASPAR LAVATER

Have you ever sat and watched the behavior of people in a public place? It can be quite educational and sometimes very amusing. To help you learn to observe behavior more objectively, I suggest that the next time you're in a public place, such as a shopping mall, airport, or doctor's office, you observe:

- how people walk—fast or slow
- how people talk—loud or quiet
- people's facial expressions—animated or controlled
- tone of voice—happy or sad, high- or low-pitched
- posture—rigid or relaxed
- eye contact—direct or indirect
- speech content—facts or feelings
- body gestures—many or few
- reaction to others—outgoing or restrained
- response under stress—angry or fearful

We all tend to partially listen to others and watch their behavior halfheartedly. We quickly move from casual observation to subjective evaluation and judgment. Many times our hasty judgments result in emotional turmoil, which produces difficult relationships and conflict between people.

The poet Robert Burns once said, "O would some power the gift to give us to see ourselves as others see us." How do your loved ones see you? Can they predict your behavior? We like to think of our own behavior as less predictable than that of others. We often think of ourselves as more complex and more difficult to understand than others. Many times we look in a mirror and see only what we want to see. Francis Quarles wrote: "If thou seest anything in thyself which may make thee proud, look a little further and thou shall find enough to humble thee; if thou be wise, view the peacock's feathers with his feet. And weigh thy best parts with thy imperfections."

The more we become aware of the behavior of others and ourselves, the more we'll be able to control our responses. Controlling our responses and reactions in our relationships will reduce tensions and help us get along better. King Solomon said, "A gentle answer turns away wrath, but harsh words cause quarrels" (Proverbs 15:1). Our behavior and our reactions to the behavior of others can positively or negatively influence our relationships.

Kinesics

The study of "body language" or "body signals" is called *kinesics*. Kinesics involves any form of body movement, including those brought about by conscious thought and those movements that are *reflexive* or involuntary. When we wave goodbye to someone, that is a *voluntary* action consciously chosen by our brain. We do, however, have many body movements or signals that aren't consciously chosen.

When we move from a dark room to a light-filled room, the pupils in our eyes automatically adjust. We don't say, "Eyes adjust!" It just happens. We can't control the immediate reaction.

Using Body Language

In learning to communicate effectively and get along with both the friendly people and the annoying people in our lives, it's important to understand body language. The various body signals of others give us clues to what they're thinking and how they're feeling. Understanding body language will help us reduce conflict and break through the defenses of family, friends, and work associates. Learning to read body signals will enhance our ability to be alert to the needs of people we come in contact with.

For many years, people have discussed the merits of an attribute commonly called "women's intuition." Some women seem to possess an uncanny ability to understand the feelings and motivations of others. Where does this unique ability come from? How are these women able to know without the obvious use of a logical thinking process? In the field of law enforcement, some police officers have the unique ability to sense when an individual is about to commit a crime. They seem to know that something is wrong or something bad is about to happen. In American slang, this intuitive knowledge is called "hinky." The police might say, "I've got a 'hinky' feeling that guy is about to sell some drugs." How do they sense this precriminal behavior?

In both these cases, neither the women nor the police officers have special, magical powers. What they're sensing, feeling, or knowing about others comes from their ability to accurately read the nonverbal behavior of the people they're observing. As a general rule, women are usually more perceptive in reading body signals than men.

This book wasn't written to be the definitive last word on body language. Hopefully, your appetite will be stirred to pursue further education on this fascinating and important topic. As you become more skilled in reading nonverbal behavior, look for *clusters* of body signals. They often communicate an overall message. An individual body gesture can be compared to a *single word* in a sentence. A grouping of body gestures can be compared to an *entire sentence*. Look for consistency, unity, and congruence.

It's possible to misread body signals if each individual signal is separated from other signals. For example, let's take the body signal of folding the arms across the chest while talking or listening to someone. This gesture, by itself, is generally considered to be a barrier or hostile gesture to openness. But what if there were other body signals accompanying the folded arms? What if the person was laughing and joking too? That would be a mixed message. You would have to keep watching to see if other signals might clarify the reason for the folded arms.

They might have their arms folded because they're cold. They might be folding their arms because someone else in the group has their arms folded. They might have a sore back, and folding their arms supports their back muscles better. They might have folded arms because they're telling a story about someone with folded arms. Now if their arms are folded, their legs are crossed, they have a frown on their face, and they are gritting their teeth, then you probably have a hostile person in front of you because the cluster of gestures is consistent.

In the study of body language, *territorial* space or zones are also important. Everyone has an *intimate space* where only special people are invited in. This might include those who are emotionally close, such as a spouse, children, other relatives, and close friends. *Personal space* expands to include fellow workers, people at parties or social functions, and salespeople. *Social space* is where people keep strangers or people they have recently met. People in this area, people are polite and friendly but a little distant and reserved at the same time. The *public space* is the area where a lot of strangers are put together as a group. This includes crowds at concerts, theaters, ball games, parks, amusement centers, and shopping malls. At these events or places, everyone is physically at the same place while being emotionally in their own worlds.

TERRITORIAL SPACES OR ZONES			
Intimate space	Personal space	Social space	Public space
6 to 18 inches	18 inches to 4 feet	4 to 12 feet	More than 12 feet

These four spaces or zones may not always be consciously on our minds. However, if someone enters an intimate or personal zone uninvited, people feel nervous, irritated, and angry. Some may even react physically by striking out. Law enforcement agencies understand territorial space very well. They know that if people are crowded together, they become hostile. The greater the density of the group, the greater the anger of the mob. Because of this, police will endeavor to break up a large group. As the crowd disperses, individuals regain their personal space. When personal space is reestablished, people become calmer.

On the reverse side, law enforcement agencies will sometimes purposefully enter people's personal or intimate spaces. They know this makes people nervous and angry. In their nervousness and anxiety, suspects will often respond with more information or won't be able to maintain a consistent storyline. The invasion of their space helps break down their defenses.

If you have difficult people in your life, try entering their personal or intimate territory without being invited. Your difficulties will immediately increase.

We've all experienced the unwritten territorial rules in our crowded society. When riding in an elevator, almost everyone watches the numbers over the door rather than looking around. Seldom do people talk to strangers on the bus or on the subway. Eye contact with others is avoided as much as possible. Staring when people have physical defects is considered off limits.

What are other rules we follow? At the theater, we put our coats on seats we're reserving for others. We put our books on the table at the library in front of the chair we want. We save spaces in lines for our friends. In public restrooms, research indicates that 90 percent of the time people choose the end toilets. Who created all of these unwritten rules? Where did they come from? How are they maintained? Basically the entire system has been created and passed on through the use of nonverbal body language.

Interesting Facts About Body Language

- In over 2,000…conflict negotiations…never once was a conflict settled where anyone in attendance had their legs crossed. Settlement was only reached when negotiators uncrossed their legs and moved toward each other.
- Mothers whose voices registered high on anxiety had daughters who were more attentive and cautious.

- Studies have shown that when a teacher's voice rises in tone and the words are rapid…classroom disruption goes up proportionately. As the teacher lowers their tone, slows their speech, and measures their words, negative classroom behavior decreases. My father taught me that long ago. He said, "If…you do that…one…more…time…you are in… trouble." End of story.

- Studies of mothers with emotionally disturbed children show that they send more conflicting verbal and nonverbal messages than mothers of normal children.

- People who live in the city shake hands with their elbows bent. They stand about eighteen inches apart. People who live in the country lean forward and shake hands with their arms fully extended and their elbows are locked. [They stand] a further distance apart.

- Wives are extremely alert to other women entering their husband's personal or intimate territory. Even if the husband is not aware of the invasion, the wife is.

- Studies indicate that a library table can be reserved by simply placing books in front of the chair at the table. This act can reserve the table up to seventy minutes. If you leave a coat on the chair it can reserve the table up to two hours.

- An individual's status can be determined by the amount of time it takes to enter a room or to answer a door. The faster a person enters the room, and the slower they answer the door…the more status they have. Employees usually do not enter their boss's office unless invited.

- One of the most irritating body gestures is to point a finger at someone. The second is to give them the "finger," a gesture from the middle of the hand.

- Individuals who are tall seem to be more successful in relationships when they decrease their height when they deal with people. They sit down in a chair or on a desk or lower themselves a little when talking to others. This helps to decrease their dominance by sheer height alone.

- Successful people seem to initiate handshaking more than unsuccessful people.

- People who are more introverted seem to keep people at a greater conversational distance than extroverts.

- People who grab their hands behind their back are showing signs of restraint. When they grab higher on their arm they are probably angry.

- When people are attempting to make guarded statements or deceive, they will often put their hand to their mouth and make a fake coughing gesture.

- When people start yawning...they usually continue to yawn from 14-17 times before they stop.

- When people put their fingers into their mouth, or other objects, it could indicate that they are feeling under pressure.

- The drumming of fingers on a table is often viewed as boredom. More likely it is a sign of impatience rather than boredom.

- A study was done on two groups of students listening to a lecture. The first group was instructed to listen with their arms crossed. The second group with their arms uncrossed. The crossed armed group retained and learned 38% less than the uncrossed arm group.

- People who are nervous will grasp on to something and hold it in front of them. If they have nothing to hold, they may grasp their own wrist or fiddle with their watch.

- On job interviews, those who are applying and have their ankles locked during the interview may be holding back something.

- When a listener's head tips slightly to the side it indicates that they are interested. Dogs also do this.

- When a person is excited their pupils will dilate up to four times their normal size. If they are angry the pupils will contract.

- Smokers who feel confident will blow their smoke upward. Those who feel negative or more depressed will blow their smoke downward.

- The more a person who smokes plays or moves their cigarette, cigar, or pipe, the more nervous they are. When they stop smoking they are probably more relaxed.

- When people begin to mirror the nonverbal behavior of the other person it is usually a compliment or a way of saying "I agree with you" or "I like you."

- When two people are talking and a third party comes up... if they point one of their toes toward them it indicates that they are accepted into the group. If not, the third party will get the message and leave.

- People whose backs are to a wall or partition show lesser heart rate and blood pressure than those whose backs are open to a doorway, window, or an open room.

- When walking toward someone there will be a meeting of the eyes. Next, there will be a very slight eye click by one or both of the parties. The eyes will either click to the right or the left. This tells the other person which way they are going to walk. When you bump into someone it is only because you did not pick up on the eye click.

- When caught looking at someone, the unwritten eye rule is for us to look away. If a woman does not look away from a man, she is giving him an invitation to approach. If the man continues to look it means that he is interested.

- When two men look at each other and do not look away it usually means trouble of some kind...and maybe even a fight might occur.

• When people lie and fail in deception of others it is usually because of one of three reasons. [1] They want to be caught. [2] They feel guilty. [3] They do not know how to monitor their own nonverbal body language.*

POINT TO PONDER

Trust not a man's words if you please, or you may come to very erroneous conclusions; but at all times place implicit confidence in a man's countenance in which there is no deceit and of necessity there can be none.

GEORGE BORROW

---

* Nierenberg and Calero, *How to Read a Person like a Book,* adapted.

13

Body Language at a Glance

He that has eyes to see and ears to hear may convince himself that no mortal can keep a secret. If his lips are silent, he chatters with his fingertips; betrayal oozes out of him at every pore.

SIGMUND FREUD

The following list of body signals or gestures are common to most people. Following each signal is the generally accepted meaning for that gesture. A review of these nonverbal behaviors will help you prepare for a confrontation (and also a job interview, performance evaluation, sales job, and dealing with people in most settings). Understanding their importance will help you communicate more effectively and know how well your message is being received. Your personal and social relationships will probably also go smoother.

- *Kissing fingertips:* Praise or salutation
- *Crossing fingers:* Good luck
- *Forefinger over lips:* Quiet please
- *Thumb to nose with fingers waving:* Mockery
- *Thumb and fingers touching with palm up:* A question or good
- *Forming a circle with thumb and first finger:* Okay or good
- *Flicking fingers under chin toward person:* Disinterest or negative
- *Thumb up:* Okay or "I agree"

- *Tapping nose with finger:* Complicity or keep a secret
- *Flicking thumb off teeth toward person:* Insult
- *Finger screwing into cheek:* Good
- *Fingers of both hands all touching each other like a steeple:* Confidence
- *Clenched fist:* Power or anger
- *Clasping hand over mouth:* "I shouldn't have said that" or shock
- *Forefinger raised:* "I've got a question" or "Excuse me"
- *Knocking on forehead:* Stubborn
- *Slapping forehead:* "How stupid of me"
- *Tapping forehead with both hands:* Crazy
- *Rubbing hands together:* Excitement or anticipation
- *Hands forming a "T":* Time out
- *Fanning mouth with fingers:* Hot
- *Tip of finger touching lip:* "I want to talk to you"
- *Picking nose:* Insult
- *Pinching nose:* "You stink" or "You make me sick"
- *Pulling lower eyelid down with finger:* "I'm watching you" or "I'm alert"
- *Punching fist into palm of other hand:* Anger or decisiveness
- *Both palms up and placed by hips:* "I swear!" or "Honest!"
- *Thumb down:* No or no good
- *Tapping both thumbnails together:* Sarcastic applause
- *Pinch cheek with finger and thumb:* Excellent
- *Forefinger moving horizontally across throat:* Threat
- *Rubbing chin:* "I don't believe you" or "Hmmm, that's interesting"
- *Chin supported in hand:* Boredom

- *Cupping hand behind ear:* "Speak up" or "I can't hear you"
- *Holding ear:* Disbelief
- *Tossing head back:* Negative response
- *Grasping other person's arm while shaking hands:* Friendliness
- *Thumbs under armpits:* Pride
- *Hands on hips with elbows sticking out from body:* "Keep away from me" or "I'm ready for action" or "I'm ready for a fight"
- *Arms folded:* Defensive
- *Both arms up with slight bend in elbow:* "I surrender"
- *Both arms reaching out in front of body:* Ready for embrace
- *Arms and hands making a shoveling motion:* Other person is talking nonsense
- *Stroking beard:* Deep in thought or "How boring"
- *Patting the belly:* "I'm full"
- *Belly pressed:* "I'm hungry"
- *Leaning forward:* Interest or paying attention
- *Sitting on the edge of chair:* About to leave or "I want out of here"
- *Legs, knees, or feet pointing toward door:* "I want out of here"
- *Supporting cheek:* "I'm tired"
- *Beating chest:* "I'm strong" or "I'm tough"
- *Hold chest with palms of hands:* "Who me?"
- *Pushing chin forward:* Threatening
- *Scratching ear:* Confusion
- *Raising eyebrows:* Greeting or flirtation or no
- *Eyes rolling back and up to stare at ceiling:* Exasperation
- *Eyes make a sideward glance:* Coyness or flirtation

- *Eyes staring directly into other person's eyes:* Threat or interest
- *Foot bouncing up and down:* Boredom
- *Locking foot behind leg:* Nervousness or discomfort
- *Showing bottom of foot to person:* Insult
- *Tapping foot up and down:* Impatience
- *Interlocking hands behind head:* Confidence or superiority or intimidation
- *Clicking heels of feet together:* Sign of respect
- *Both hands on knees while sitting:* "I'm going to leave" or "I want out of here"
- *Crossing leg and grasping it with one or both hands:* Stubborn
- *Stroking leg:* "I think you're attractive"
- *Crossing of leg with ankle on the knee:* "I'm confident and relaxed"
- *Crossing of leg with knee over knee:* Very relaxed
- *Biting of lower lip:* Anger or girl being coy
- *Mimic sealing or zipping lips:* "Keep quiet" or "Don't say a word"
- *Biting fingernails:* Nervous or anxious
- *Grabbing back of neck with hand:* "I'm upset" or angry
- *Shrugging shoulders with both palms up:* "I'm innocent" or "I don't know"
- *Sticking out tongue:* Insult or "I don't like you"
- *Smile without showing teeth:* Probably smiling to self
- *Smile showing upper teeth:* Used in meeting people
- *Smile with mouth open showing upper and lower teeth:* Happy and playful
- *Smile that is oblong without showing teeth:* Polite smile
- *Smile that is oblong with teeth showing:* Pain

- *Walking with shoulders bent forward and in:* Sadness or depression
- *Walking with hands on hips:* Energy
- *Walking back and forth:* Nervous or energetic or excitement or deep in thought or attempting to make a point or needing to go to the bathroom
- *Walking with hands behind back:* Deep in thought
- *Sitting with leg over arm of chair:* Hostility or indifference
- *Straddling chair with chair back in front of chest:* Dominance
- *Sitting with forefinger near side of head or side of nose:* Evaluation
- *Looking over the top of eyeglasses:* "I don't believe you" or "Would you repeat that?"
- *Pen or eyeglasses earpiece in mouth:* Evaluation or possible dishonesty
- *Both hands on table while body leans toward others:* "This is a showdown"
- *Tugging at pants while sitting:* A decision is being made
- *Hand covering mouth with forefinger touching nose:* Possible dishonesty
- *Forefinger over lips while talking:* Not sure of what they are saying or possible dishonesty

POINT TO PONDER

Look in the face of the person to whom you are speaking if you wish to know his real sentiments, for he can command his words more easily than his countenance.

LORD CHESTERFIELD

14

Listening to Reduce Conflict

*Everyone should be quick to listen, slow to
speak and slow to become angry.*

JAMES, BROTHER OF JESUS, JAMES 1:19

Kurt, may I talk to you for a minute?" Amber had cornered him
just as he was walking out of the conference room. She was a little perturbed with him after he'd dismissed one of her ideas in a recent
company brainstorming meeting.

"Uh, okay…I guess so. What's up, Amber?" Kurt was in a hurry and
didn't particularly want to deal with Amber right now. They'd been
experiencing tension in their relationship. Amber seemed to spread
negativity throughout the organization, and Kurt would rather avoid
her.

"Can we go into your office, Kurt? I have something I want to discuss with you."

"Sure." Kurt sighed heavily and led the way. Amber followed him
into his office, and they both sat down.

Kurt thumbed through his messages while Amber mustered up the
nerve to say what was on her mind. She wrung her hands as she talked.

"I just wanted to tell you how frustrated I was in that last meeting.
As soon as I started to share my idea, you cut me off and dismissed my
input like it didn't matter. It seemed like…"

"I wasn't trying to demean your input, Amber." Kurt cut in before
she finished her sentence. "I already knew how you felt about my proposal, and I didn't want you to spread your negativity."

"What is that supposed to mean?" Amber leaned back and crossed her arms over her chest.

"It means that you're very negative. I knew if you started in, you would turn other people against my idea. I didn't want—"

Amber cut him off before he could finish. "Stop right there, Kurt. That's a crock—and you know it. Just because I want people to look at all sides of the issue doesn't make me negative. You think everyone should see it your way or—"

Kurt jumped in and started talking over Amber's voice. "You're doing it right now! You just look at the negative side of everything—and it's annoying!"

"Well, you just cut me off for the third time today, which you do constantly. I can't talk to you!" Amber stood up and stormed out of the room.

"Good riddance!" Kurt mumbled under his breath as he rose, walked over, and slammed the door behind her.

POINT TO PONDER

When we are in conflict, there is always at least one thing we share with our opponents: We both know we are right!

KENNETH CLOKE

Unfortunately, this type of exchange is very common. When people attempt to resolve conflict, they often hold strongly to their own positions. When they feel their position is being violated or invalidated, they defend it even more. One of the fastest ways to invalidate someone's position, idea, or view is to refuse to listen. King Solomon said, "Fools find no pleasure in understanding but delight in airing their own opinions" (Proverbs 18:2 NIV).

Cutting people off or interrupting them while they're talking is a common practice that escalates conflict. People will raise their voices to be heard or completely withdraw in rebellion to the invalidation. So we need to stop and ask ourselves, "Is the goal here to prove I'm right or is the goal to resolve the conflict and have all parties feel validated in being heard?"

POINT TO PONDER

When we demonize our opponents, we also label and stereotype them; find evil in their hearts; and sincerely come to believe that they are unjust, dishonest, disagreeable, untrustworthy personalities. We personalize their behaviors toward us, even when their actions clearly have more to do with *their* perceptions, emotions, and unresolved issues than with us.

KENNETH CLOKE

If you're standing across the room and you say something to someone and they can't hear you, what do you do? Normally, you talk louder. If someone is across the street and they can't hear you, you shout to them until they can. Well, that's also how people respond in conflict. If they bring up an issue and they feel they're not being heard or listened to, they'll talk louder. If they still feel they're not being heard, they'll shout. Sometimes the shouting is *passive* in nature and consists of complete withdrawal from the situation. Sometimes the shouting is *literal* as voices are raised and tempers flare.

Active Listening

One of the keys to reducing conflict is "to hear and be heard." How is that done? Very carefully! "Active listening" takes a tremendous amount of energy and patience. When used properly, it builds bridges and reduces conflicts tremendously. When people feel heard, they don't feel the need to demand additional recognition of their point or position later.

Do you consider yourself a good listener?

An old man goes to his doctor and says, "I don't think my wife's hearing is as good as it used to be. What should I do?"

The doctor replies, "Try this test to find out for sure. When your wife is in the kitchen doing dishes, stand fifteen feet behind her and ask her a question. If she doesn't respond, keep moving closer, asking the question until she hears you."

The man goes home and sees his wife preparing dinner. He stands fifteen feet behind her and says, "What's for dinner, honey?" No response. He moves to ten feet behind her and asks again. No response. He moves within five feet, and asks, "Honey, what's for dinner?"

Still no answer.

Finally he stands directly behind her and says, "Honey, what's for dinner?"

She turns abruptly and shouts, "For the fourth time, *I said chicken!*"

Most people think they're great listeners, and it's everyone else who has the problem. While many people feel they listen well, few really do. Listening isn't merely sitting quietly and allowing someone to rant and rave about their feelings or a particular issue. Listening isn't tapping your foot while you anxiously wait for the person to finish their sentence so you can give your view. Listening isn't thinking about your response or comeback while the other person is spilling their guts. Listening isn't being quiet while someone talks...but thinking about what you have to do tomorrow. Listening isn't remaining silent while someone talks as you divide your attention between them and the papers on your desk.

Active listening takes work. It takes commitment. Listening is hard enough when everything is going smoothly, but it's even more difficult when conflict is involved. Not only does it take energy to listen carefully, but it also takes energy to not become defensive yourself. It takes effort to control your own temper and stay calm. It takes control to not jump to conclusions. Listening requires patience.

Attentive listening is an act of kindness, an act of caring. It takes concentration. You have to *deliberately* turn the focus from your own thoughts and emotions to those of the person you're talking to. You have to listen as if you were in their shoes and walking their path.

Active listening goes beyond receiving the intended message. You also let the people know they are heard. The first step in active listening is giving your *undivided attention* to the person who is speaking. This means not multitasking while the people are talking. The best communication is done in person, but sometimes issues need to be dealt with over the phone. When someone is talking over the phone about an issue, it's easy to get sidetracked and do other things while the person is talking because you don't have to make eye contact with them. Resist this urge. Give your full attention to the speaker so you can completely absorb the true message and emotions being shared.

If you're communicating with someone in person, give that person your undivided attention. As a listener, become conscious of your own behaviors that may distract from the listening process. Do you fiddle with pencils or keys? Do you jingle money in your pocket, fidget, or drum your fingers on a nearby surface. These behaviors don't help you or the others in the listening process. Cracking knuckles, frequently shifting weight, crossing and uncrossing legs, swinging legs up and down, watching TV across the room, or waving and nodding to other people going by sends a negative message to the speaker. It says, "I'm not really interested."

To be an effective listener, you often have to sacrifice time. You have to decline phone calls, get off the computer, set aside other work while the other person speaks. Your workload may increase as you exercise the difficult task of active listening.

Eye contact is also very important. You need to focus on the speaker and what is being said. Have you spoken to people who look past you? You can't tell if they're bored, wanting to talk to someone else, or simply aren't interested. When you make consistent eye contact with the person talking to you, you're saying, "I'm listening to you." An old adage says, "If you loan a man your ears, you immediately open a pathway to his heart."

Make sure your eyes are on the same level as the person talking. If you stand up and look down on the person, you may project a negative sense of domination or power. If you're sitting and the other person is standing, you may experience the same effect in reverse. Level eye contact lends itself to a more cohesive listening environment and keeps everyone on more equal footing in the conversation.

Now that you're providing your undivided attention and maintaining good eye contact, *listen*. This means your mouth and your mind are both quiet while you process what the person is saying to you. Your mind can't properly assess the intended message if it's busy racing about with other thoughts.

As the person speaks, your own emotions may rise or frustration may emerge. The person may make generalizations, such as "You always..." or "You never..." Although the person communicating may exaggerate the situation or describe it differently than you see it, remain calm and attentive. This is a tempting time for you to cut the person off and set the record straight. This is a tempting time to correct the areas where you believe the person is blatantly wrong. As hard as it may be, resist this temptation. Listen to the *entire* message.

This is probably the most difficult stage in the listening process for most people. A nagging urge to jump in usually overcomes the listener. The "listener" interrupts, and the person who was talking feels invalidated and becomes more adamant about the problem. Even in casual conversation, interrupting is rude because it sends a message to other people that you believe what you have to say is much more important than what they have to share. It tells people you don't value their thoughts or ideas...or even them.

POINT TO PONDER

You will be far more successful in resolving your disputes when you stop debating endlessly over who is to blame for the past and instead focus on how to solve your problems in the present or what you both want for the future.

KENNETH CLOKE

People often use excuses for interrupting. "I'm just trying to add to the conversation." "I was just interjecting a quick clarification." "If I didn't say something, I would have forgotten." "Well, you talk too long. I have things to say too." "You cut me off too!" There's really no good excuse for interrupting people or finishing their sentences. If you want to send a message that you value the opinion of others, you really have to listen and let them know they are heard.

Having said that, if you're the talker, don't abuse people's willingness to listen to you. Take little breaks and allow them to share their thoughts and feelings as well.

Now that you're giving your undivided attention, you're making good eye contact, and you're listening without interrupting, you can begin to "reflect back." This is the next important step in the active listening process.

What Is "Reflecting Back"?

After you've given people the opportunity to really speak their minds, allow yourself a moment to absorb all that was said. Instead of immediately telling your side of the issue, take the time to let the people know you heard what was said. This takes a little more than just saying, "Okay, I heard you. Now you get to hear me." Letting them know they've really been listened to takes a process referred to as "reflecting back." When you reflect back to someone, you express back to them what you heard them say. This confirms that you received the message the person wanted you to receive. It gives the other party an opportunity to clarify details, if needed, so everyone is on the same page. People are much more likely to be receptive to new views and positions when they feel they've been heard, their message has been understood, and their input has been considered in the resolution process.

Let's go back to the conversation between Amber and Kurt. Remember, Kurt interrupted Amber in the meeting, cutting her off because of her negativity. Let's look at how reflecting back would have looked like. Amber started out with, "I wanted to tell you how frustrated I was in that last meeting. As soon as I started to share my idea, you cut me off and dismissed my input like it didn't matter. It seems like—" At that point, Kurt cut her off, which frustrated Amber even more. She then proceeded to cut him off, and the conflict escalated, with both of them talking at the same time. If Kurt had practiced active listening and reflecting back, the conversation may have been more productive.

> *Amber:* "I wanted to tell you how frustrated I was in that last meeting. As soon as I started to share my idea, you cut me off and dismissed my input like it didn't matter. It seems like you don't care what I think. I had some really good ideas I wanted to add, and you passed right over me. That really hurt my feelings, Kurt."

> *Kurt after a short pause:* "If I understand you correctly, you feel like I wasn't listening to your ideas and just cut you off. That made you feel like your opinion didn't matter to me, and I hurt your feelings. It sounds like you're annoyed with me. Is that correct?"

> *Amber:* "Yes, that's exactly what I'm feeling. I'm sure you weren't trying to be mean, but it feels like you haven't been open to my input lately."

> *Kurt:* "So you also feel like I've been negating your input in some other areas as well? And you feel frustrated with me. Is that right?"

> *Amber:* "Yes, that's how I've been feeling."

At this point, Kurt hasn't agreed with Amber or told her she's correct or she's wrong. He hasn't indicated any judgment on the situation or defended his position. He's simply listened and made sure Amber knew she was heard. He's told her that her intended message was received and understood.

Now that Amber has felt heard, she'll probably be more open to listening to Kurt's viewpoint and use her active listening skills too.

> *Kurt:* "I can understand why you might be feeling that way. I did cut you off and dismiss your input in the meeting. I didn't mean to be rude. It's just that I knew you were

already against my proposal, and I thought you would turn everyone else against it. I've been avoiding your input in other areas somewhat because I've felt you might shoot them down too. It seems like you approach some of the ideas around here with a very critical eye."

Amber: "I hear you saying you feel like I would have turned everyone against your idea in the meeting. That's why you didn't let me finish my input. Is that right?"

Kurt: "Yes, that's right."

Amber: "And you also feel like I've been pretty negative about other ideas lately?"

Kurt: "Yes. I'm sure you just want to be sure everything gets done right, but sometimes it comes across as negativity."

Amber: "I can see where it might come across that way. I'll try harder to present my input in a more positive way. I'd appreciate it if you would let me share my ideas without cutting me off, especially in meetings. I think we both have a lot to offer in the way of these brainstorming sessions. If we both let the other share fully, our coworkers will know we respect each other. That will make the meetings less stressful for everyone."

Kurt: "I think that's fair. Thanks for coming and sharing your concerns with me."

Then they both stood up and hugged.

Okay, maybe that's taking it too far, but at least one of them didn't go stomping out of the office in a rage and the other didn't slam the door. Active listening really does work. After each person thoroughly listened to the other and then relayed back, both gained validation and understanding. If you want people to hear and understand you, you have to be willing to first hear them and understand their position. When you do that, walls of resistance come down, fighting stops, and bridges are built.

What are some good openings for reflective statements?

"Are you saying..."   "Little things?"

"As I get it..."   "Problems?"

"Great things?"   "Stuff like?"

"I get the feeling that..." "Weird?"

"In other words..."   "You believe..."

"Interesting?"   "You want to..."

Reflective statements might include "clarification questions" like these:

"Am I safe to assume that you mean...?"

"Help me out. I'm not sure I understand what you're saying."

"I hear you saying...but I'm not sure what you mean. Will you explain this further?"

"I think I hear you saying... Am I understanding you correctly?"

"I'm totally confused. Will you explain this again?"

"Let me share with you my impressions so far, and you let me know if we're on the same page."

"Will you please tell me more about...?"

Clarification statements or questions are expressed in a tentative manner. This way the speaker won't feel challenged or defensive and will readily clear up any misunderstandings. It lets them know you're listening carefully to their concerns.

Reflecting Back Reduces Communication Conflicts

Conflicts often arise out of miscommunication. Someone said something that was interpreted a completely different way. Keep your messages clear and make sure your intended message is received and understood.

A couple showed up at a very popular restaurant. It was crowded, and there was a long line of people waiting. The husband approached the maître d' and asked, "Will it be long?"

The maître d' kept writing in her book and didn't look up.

The husband asked again, "How much of a wait can we expect?"

The woman finally looked up and said, "About twenty minutes."

A short time later, an announcement came over the loudspeaker: "Willette B. Long, your table is ready."

What you intended to communicate isn't always the message that was received. While in some cases this can be humorous, in other cases it can cause a great deal of conflict. When you "relay back," you're repeating the message and asking for confirmation or clarification. Clear and concise communication is a critical aspect of any cohesive relationship.

A judge was interviewing a woman regarding her pending divorce. He asked, "What are the grounds for your divorce?"

She replied, "About four acres and a nice little home in the middle of the property with a stream running by."

"No," the judge said. "I mean, What is the foundation of your case?"

"It's made of concrete, brick, and mortar," she responded.

"I mean," the judge corrected, "what are your relations like?"

"I have an aunt and uncle living here in town, and my husband's parents live here too."

The judge took a deep breath. "Do you have a real grudge?"

"No," she replied. "We have a two-car carport and have never really needed anything more."

"Please," the judge begged.

"Is there any infidelity in your marriage?"

"Yes. Both my son and daughter have stereos. We don't necessarily like the music, but the answer to your question is yes."

"Ma'am, does your husband ever beat you up?"

"Yes," she responded. "About twice a week he gets up earlier than I do."

Finally, in full frustration, the judge asked, "Lady, why do you want a divorce?"

"Oh, I don't want a divorce," she replied. "I've never wanted a divorce. My husband does. He said he can't communicate with me."

Communication is a two-way street—and it doesn't just require talking and listening. It also requires understanding. Reflecting back helps bridge any gaps of misunderstanding and allows time and room for clarifications.

POINT TO PONDER

Our conflicts are our teachers and liberators because they invite us to wake up and become aware of what we have not yet learned how to handle skillfully. As Carl Jung wrote, "Everything that irritates us about others can lead us to an understanding of ourselves."

KENNETH CLOKE

General Tips for Active Listening

One of the things that will help you become a better listener is to be more alert to the emotions that are stirred when someone is talking. These emotions give us clues to the messages that are being conveyed by the speaker. This means being aware of negative feelings and positive feelings. To the best of your ability, you need to understand the message and emotions of the speaker and yourself at the same time.

Words for Describing Emotions

To help you explore communicating emotions, see the two lists on the following pages. The first is "Positive Emotion Words." The second is "Negative Emotion Words." Study them so you can be more fluent in your descriptions of what you hear other people saying and what you want to say when talking about your own emotions during the active listening process.

Setting the Stage for Positive Communication

Be aware of your body posture. Lean slightly forward and face the speaker squarely. Maintain an "open" position with your arms not folded. Position yourself an appropriate distance from the speaker so both of you are comfortable.

Create a non-distracting environment. Turn off the TV or stereo. Close the door to your office to prevent interruptions. Remove any physical barriers, such as plants, desks, lamps, etc. If you're in a place where you could be disturbed it might be good to go for a walk and talk.

Open the door for communication. You might start with a comment like "Your face is beaming today" or "You look like you're not feeling up to par." Invite the person to share or to continue speaking by saying, "Care to talk about it?" or "Please go on" or "I'm interested in what you're saying."

Short responses encourage sharing. Often a short response of one to three words will help open communication and encourage the speaker to proceed. These responses don't imply either agreement or disagreement with the speaker. They do let the speaker know you're following the conversation and are interested. You're encouraging the speaker to continue. Some samples are:

"And?"	"So?"
"For instance..."	"Sure."
"Go on."	"Tell me more."
"I see."	"Then?"
"Oh!"	"Wow!"
"Really?"	"Yes."

POSITIVE EMOTION WORDS

Admired
Important
Looked up to
Respected

Alive
Animated
Bubbly
Buoyant
Effervescent
Invigorated
Vibrant
Vivacious

Anticipating
Eager

Approved
Acceptable
Accepted
Appreciated
Respected
Supported
Sustained

Calm
At peace
Composed
Peaceful
Safe
Secure
Serene
Tranquil

Concerned
Caring

Confident
Adequate
Capable
Competent

Considered
Included
Understood

Elated
Cheered
Encouraged
Hopeful
Inspired
Joyful

Optimistic
Positive

Fulfilled
At peace
Comfortable
Enriched
Gratified
Pleased
Satisfied
Worthy

Inspired
Enlightened
Impressed
Uplifted

Needed
Cared for
Loved
Protected
Wanted

Relieved
At ease
Consoled

Romantic
Sentimental
Thoughtful

Sensitive
Feeling

Sincere
In earnest

Stimulated
Cheerful
Chipper
Happy
Invigorated
Refreshed
Renewed
Revitalized

Supported
Sustained

Worthy
Accepted
Deserving
Trusted

NEGATIVE EMOTION WORDS

Abandoned
Deserted
Isolated
Shut out
Alienated
Rejected
Left out
Severed
Cut off
Shunned
Forsaken
Alone
Excluded

Anxious
Uneasy
Frightened
Scared
Afraid
Fearful
Alarmed
Panicked
Terrified

Burden
Endured
Tolerated
Appeased
Patronized
In the way
Put up with

Cold
Lukewarm
Unfeeling

Uncaring
Careless
Callous

Confused
Mixed up
Baffled
Bewildered
Perplexed
Disoriented

Deprived
Devastated
Spent
Drained
Wasted

Disappointed
Let down
Dejected
Discouraged
Deflated

Dominated
Used
Managed
Exploited
Imposed upon
Cheated
Burdened
Saddled

Edgy
Restless

Foolish
Shamed

Embarrassed
Mocked

Frustrated
Thwarted
Stifled
Cornered
Trapped
Caged

Humiliated
Deflated
Degraded
Debased
Belittled
Underrated
Criticized
Defeated
Put down
Shot down

Injured
Resentful
Furious
Indignant

Offended
Provoked
Harassed
Hassled
Annoyed

Overwhelmed
Smothered
Oppressed

Shocked
Surprised
Amazed
Appalled
Stunned

Threatened
Invaded

Unconcerned
Indifferent
Detached
Bored

Unloved
Unwanted
Unwelcome
Ignored

Upset
Bothered
Agitated
Uptight
Distressed
Worried
Troubled
Torn
Frantic

Wary
Suspicious
Untrusting

Strategic questions open up conversation. When you ask questions endeavor to keep them open-ended. This basically means asking questions that can't be answered with a simple "yes" or "no" statement. It's helpful to form your questions in such a way as to encourage the other people to carefully consider before they answer and assume responsibility for their conclusion. "If you tell your boss off, how do you think that will affect your job with the company?" Reflective questions help people evaluate their own motives, ideas, and behavior. It helps them clarify their thinking.

Also, only ask one question at a time. Allow the speaker to answer each one. Don't overload the person by asking several questions at the same time. This will help keep the conversation focused and avoid getting sidetracked by running down less important "rabbit trails."

If the speaker asks questions, actively listen. Determine if the question is really a true question. Sometimes people "attack by question": "You never do what I want to do...do you?" This not a true question. It's really a statement with a question mark at the end. "Where were you last night?" is often a statement of judgment or anger. It can be a veiled approach to say they're disappointed you were late or didn't show up.

"What are you doing tomorrow afternoon?"...may not be asked because people want to know your schedule. They may really want to find out if you'll give them a ride to the shopping center.

"What time is it?"...may be asked for another reason besides wanting to know the hour and minutes. The speaker might be bored at a party and want to go home.

"How much did you pay?"...might be asked because the speaker thinks you paid too much or you didn't pay enough.

I was at a friend's house one day when his wife said, "Are you going to comb your hair?"

I smiled and said, "Why didn't you tell him to hurry up and get ready or we're going to be late?"

She responded, "I didn't want to come right out and say that."

I said, "But you did."

Just because a sentence has a question mark at the end doesn't mean that it is a true question.

POINT TO PONDER

It can be stated with practically no qualification that people in general do not know how to listen. For several years, we have been testing the ability of people to understand and remember what they hear...These extensive tests led to this general conclusion: immediately after the average person has listened to someone talk, he remembers only about half of what he has heard—no matter how carefully he thought he was listening. What happens as time passes: Our testing shows...that we tend to forget from one-half to one-third [more] within eight hours.

DR. RALPH G. NICHOLS,
UNIVERSITY OF MINNESOTA

Silence is your friend. Sometimes it's best to just be quiet. Silence gives the other person time to decide whether to talk or not. It gives them time to pull their thoughts together and proceed at their own pace. Don't be afraid of silence. You don't have to fill in the gaps with talk. Silence often serves as a gentle nudge to go deeper into the conversation. Your eye contact and body posture demonstrate your interest and concern for the speaker. Be silent and observe. Silence can be an effective means of gaining additional information.

> Susan asks, "Charlie, we're missing a file from the classified file drawer. Do you know anything about it?"
>
> "I work in a different department."
>
> Susan stays silent. She nods her head a few times, encouraging Charlie to share more. Most people become nervous when there is silence, especially if they have something to be nervous about.
>
> Charlie volunteers, "I rarely go over to the classified area."
>
> Susan remains silent and looks at Charlie thoughtfully, without accusation.

Charlie adds, "I was only in the classified area one time last week."

Often when a story comes out by bits and pieces, it's because the speaker is trying to hide something. Their nervousness will keep them talking and watching the questioner until they think they have them convinced everything is fine.

Listen with concern. Remember that *everyone has a story.* Part of your task is to find out what is going on in the other people's lives. Why do they have the concerns they're expressing? Why are they displaying such strong emotions now, and what has caused them? Professional counselors basically ask these three strategic questions:

- What is going on?
- How do you feel about it?
- Do you want to change?

Look for any patterns that may be emerging. Is this a recurring situation in their lives? Has this happened before? If so, how did they handle it then?

Also be aware of your own attitudes during the conflict communication process. Ask these questions:

- Am I affected by their political position?
- Am I reacting to their religious convictions?
- Am I struggling with an age, gender, or race issue?
- Am I disagreeing with their lifestyles or attitudes?
- Am I judging their physical appearance, social standing, or education background?

In the process of active listening, ask yourself these questions:

- Does what they're saying make sense?
- Is what they're saying believable?
- Is what they're saying aligning with known information?

- Do their words and body language agree or disagree?
- Are their emotions out of proportion for the event going on?
- If there is something else going on, what might it be?
- How will their thoughts, words, or behavior affect the conflict situation?
- Will they make the situation better or worse?
- What is my role in what is going on?
- What do they want from me specifically?
- How can I help?

Taking notes will help you now and later. Make notes before, during, and after the discussion if possible. These notes can be either written or mental. The purpose is to remember questions or comments you'd like to make. These may include clarifications of facts so there will be no misunderstandings. By writing down thoughts immediately after a discussion, you have information to refer to, an opportunity to ask for clarification, and a record of what has transpired and when.

POINT TO PONDER

One of the first things that every top executive learns is that a very high percentage of his salary goes just to pay him or her to listen.

Listening carefully often reveals deceit. If you were to say to someone, "Good to see you," they might reply by saying, "Good to see you too." This would be a normal response. They are playing back the same words to you.

When people are asked a question and they respond by using the same words *and adding a negative*, they *might not* be telling the truth.

Question: "Did you steal my wallet?"

Answer: "No, I did not steal your wallet." [They might be involved.]

Question: "Did you hit your brother?"

Answer 1: "I didn't do it." [They're probably telling the truth.]

Answer 2: "I did not hit my brother." [The odds are they hit their brother.]

If people are asked a question like "Did you take a computer from the warehouse?," they might become very defensive. They might say things like "How dare you ask me that!" "Don't you trust me?" "I think you've got it in for me." They could go into an emotional tirade. If that happens, be careful not to accept their response at face value. Their over-defensiveness might be a dead giveaway of their guilt. Remember what Shakespeare wrote in *Hamlet,* "The lady doth protest too much, methinks."

When people mumble or speak softly, it may indicate they're hiding something. It could also mean they have a low self-image.

Be a little suspicious of those who say things like "to be frank," "to tell the truth," and "to be perfectly honest." When a person is honest and telling the truth, he or she doesn't have to announce the fact continually. When a person does, it could be a set-up for something not true.

You might also be wise to question the truth of the speaker if the story sounds rehearsed. Anyone who has a host of details about a situation, and they can recite them in complete order at the drop of a hat, has obviously been thinking about the answer for quite a while.

Often in a court of law in the United States, especially in days gone by, witnesses are asked, "Do you solemnly swear to tell the truth, the whole truth, and nothing but the truth, so help you God?"

Do you solemnly swear to tell the truth. This covers lies of commission. Deliberate lying in an attempt to deceive.

The whole truth. To be honest about all the facts. Not leaving anything out that's important. Leaving out important facts is a way to deceive.

And nothing but the truth. This covers "lies of influence." Lies of influence are attempts to "muddy the waters" by adding information to derail the questioners when they're getting too close to the truth.

So help you God? This is an appeal to a standard by which truth is measured. It's an attempt to keep people honest by making them feel guilty and fearful if they lie. They need to understand that God will be aware of their lies, and there will be eternal consequences if they don't tell the truth.

Be alert to those who are stalling for time. They may be assessing which way to mislead or protect themselves.

- "Why would you ask a question like that?"
- "Who told you that information?"
- "What are you driving at?"
- "Could you be more specific?"
- "Well, that is a complicated subject."

Don't be misled from the point of the conversation by those who use humor or sarcasm. They can be techniques used to confuse or avoid facing uncomfortable questions. Just smile and say, "That's a humorous story. Now, can we return to the question?"

Watch out for the "dump truck." Another way people avoid uncomfortable issues or questions is to overload the questioner with a dump truck full of information. Useless facts and details may delay the questioner from getting too close to the true issue.

GENERAL RULE #1

If the speaker lies at any point, he or she may have lied about everything else.

GENERAL RULE #2

Innocent people usually answer quickly and casually. Guilty people want to know why you're asking the questions and where you're getting your facts. They want to know how much you know so they can cover their backsides. They want to keep their stories straight and consistent. Remember the adage, "You don't have to have a good memory if you always tell the truth."

GENERAL RULE #3

If emotions are out of proportion for the situation or event, something else is going on. What is it?

GENERAL RULE #4

Don't lay all your cards on the table first. Get all available information *before* you give your information. Save your aces (your most important facts or details) for last. For example, you might ask, "Is there anything else you want to get off your chest?" This question is very powerful. The speaker may be caught a little off guard and, because of nervousness, relay additional information.

Listening can be part of the healing process. Listening with your "inner ear" (your heart) helps decrease anger-based emotions. It helps clarify and clear-up misunderstandings. It helps keep conversations on track and builds relationships.

Listening with your inner ear will help you be a more effective spouse, parent, friend, and leader. Your communication skills will increase and you'll be more able to successfully resolve conflicts at home, work, and in your community.

POINT TO PONDER

A good listener is not only popular everywhere, but after a while he knows something.

WILSON MIZNER

Active Listening Takes Practice

Active listening is not the easiest thing to do in the world. It takes time, patience, and—most of all—practice. If you have a habit of cutting people off, interrupting, or interjecting, it will take time to break that habit. When you replace the old habit with active listening skills, you'll begin to see more positive behavior patterns emerge.

If you have a habit of becoming overly defensive or clamming up during conflicts, you'll need practice before you'll feel comfortable using your new active listening skills, including relaying back information. Don't give up because it feels awkward or time consuming.

Active listening requires setting aside pride and stubbornness and exercising patience and understanding. This will be much easier for the Amiables and Analyticals than for the Drivers and the Expressives. Amiables and Analyticals are natural "askers," and they are more patient by nature. It's much easier for them not to cut people off and to listen intently. The challenge for these two social styles is to resist the temptation to either avoid the confrontation or withdraw from it. They must also resist the temptation to be stubborn and clam up. The challenges for Drivers and Expressives are to listen patiently and not interrupt. They are natural "tellers." They are more than willing to do the confronting, but they struggle with the listening part. They'll share their thoughts and feelings freely, but sitting still and absorbing from others are challenges.

As you begin to apply active listening skills, you'll notice reduced levels of conflict around you. You'll also notice that conflicts don't escalate as quickly, nor do they become as volatile. Active listening says you care, and when people believe you care, bridges of trust are built. Strong bridges of trust are much more likely to withstand inevitable conflicts than weak, rickety ones. Active listening will pave the way to constructive conflict resolutions and a more peaceful existence.

15

Dealing with
Responses to Conflict

*Conflict can be an opportunity for growth or a
tool for the destruction of relationships.*

W hen you confront someone, there are a variety of possible
responses you may experience. The most common one is *defensiveness*. Here are seven often-used defensive tactics:

1. They may refuse to discuss the issue with you. They won't
   give you the time of day. This is basically an out-of-sight
   out-of-mind move.

2. They may demonstrate selective hearing. They'll hear
   only what they want to hear. They'll focus on one of your
   possible misstatements or incorrect facts. They'll make
   that a major issue so you can't get to the heart of the matter.
   It's a diversion. This is an "overpower the confronter with
   words" move.

3. They'll let you know you're not perfect. They'll bring up
   your faults to divert away from the pressure they're feeling.
   This is a "turn the tables on you" move.

4. They give a host of excuses concerning the confrontation.
   These smokescreens are used to confuse the issue. They'll
   endeavor to convince you that their excuses are valid, and
   you need to change your mind about the issue. This is a
   "confuse the enemy" move.

5. They will reject and not accept any points of the confrontation. This is a "straightforward power play" move.

6. They will triangle others into the situation by attempting to get other people on their side. They want to apply social pressure against you. This is a "power in numbers" move.

7. They will immediately agree with you. "Yes, you are right and I am wrong." This is an attempt to placate you in the hopes that you will back off and they won't have to change. This is a "clever and subtle deception" move.

Moderation and "Tone Scaling"

Whenever any tactic is used to avoid conflict or confrontation, it is usually done in an effort to avoid taking ownership of the problem. For instance, Kara confronted Collin about an issue at work. Every time she tried to address the issue, he would use a different tactic to avoid taking ownership. Kara had to continue to bring him back to the issue until he finally took ownership.

"Collin, I need to talk to you. I've noticed that you've been coming in late every day for the past week. I need you to be here on time."

"Well, I keep getting stuck in traffic. It's not my fault." Collin was already defensive.

"Then I need you to leave earlier so you can get here on time," Kara responded.

"Mike was late last week, and no one made a big deal out of it." Collin offered up a second tactic.

"I'm not talking about Mike's behavior. I'm talking about yours. I need you to be here on time and stop coming in late." Kara was bringing Collin back to the primary issue.

"I have been working really hard! I stayed an extra hour yesterday. Does anyone notice when I do something right?" Collin continued to deflect ownership of the problem.

"Collin, you're an excellent employee. This has nothing to do with that. This issue is about one area of your current behavior—being late for work. I would rather you got here on time instead of staying late. You're setting an example for other employees too." Kara could feel her patience being tested.

"You're right," Collin finally relented. "I need to get here on time, and I will make sure I do that. I'm sorry for arguing with you about it. I've just had a tough two weeks."

This type of exchange is very common. People initially get defensive and will attempt to redirect the attention elsewhere instead of taking ownership. With effective confrontation, you must patiently bring the person back to the issue until ownership is admitted and accepted. The following chart shows how a high level of defensiveness makes it difficult for someone to take ownership. As time elapses and defensiveness drops, the chances of someone owning the problem increases. Successful confrontation and resolution takes a tremendous amount of patience.

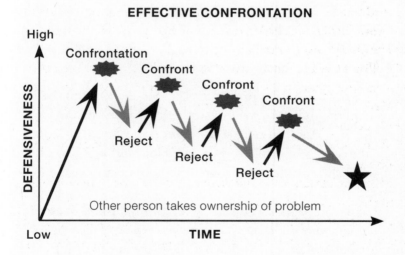

EFFECTIVE CONFRONTATION

There will be situations during this process where emotions will run high and the people being confronted may get upset. They may raise their voices as they become more defensive. They may also move to an offensive role in an effort to avoid taking ownership by putting you on the defensive.

The best guide is to keep the discussions at a moderate intensity level. The increase of pitch, tonal quality, and volume in voices will often cause discussions to escalate. The most ideal plan is to speak softly and gently. As Proverbs 15:1 says, "A gentle answer turns away wrath."

In the cases where voice volume and emotions run high, you may need to exercise "tone scaling." This technique is used to keep conflict from escalating out of control. When the other party's voice goes up, your voice parallels theirs. This raising of your voice doesn't mean you're losing control or ready to start an outright fight. On the contrary, raising your voice is done to let the other party know that...

- you are not afraid of them.
- you are not going to be bullied by them.
- you are not going to back down from them.
- you are not going to let their negative behavior continue unaddressed.
- you are not going to run from the conflict and the matters to be discussed.
- you are here to deal with the issue.

In tone scaling, you rise to their level of tone and remain there for a time until they become aware you are serious. Then you can lower your voice to your normal range and measure your words. This is done to help the other person follow your lead. Hopefully their voice will also lower. When that happens, more significant discussion and resolution can occur.

If that doesn't happen, you need to be alert to the nearest exit. In all seriousness, tone scaling is a very effective method of meeting with a highly emotional person. It addresses where they are in their feeling level. It can help them realize where they are and provide assistance to move them to a point where more meaningful conversation can occur.

Whether dealing with the public, coworkers, family, or friends, confrontation will always be a challenge. People won't always respond as you may expect or desire. Your "hot issue" buttons may get pushed, and you may not react as they expect and you would like. Learning how to

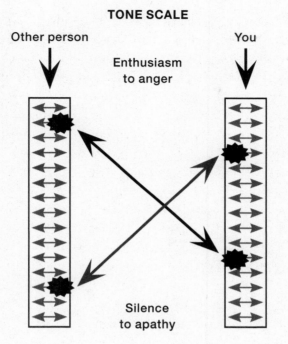

deal with confrontation and conflict will help facilitate stronger, more cohesive relationships in your life.

POINT TO PONDER

In every conflict, the past weighs heavily on the present. This is especially true in conflict-avoidant organizations, those where conflicts are routinely suppressed, denied, settled, and incompletely resolved. In these organizations, conflicts are allowed to fester and multiply, or they are isolated, shunned, and sidelined. More often, they are passed on to others through gossip and rumors and are nursed and hoarded, sometimes for lifetimes.

KENNETH CLOKE

16

When You're the One Confronted

*No man resolved to make the most of himself can spare
time for personal contention. Still less can he afford to
take all the consequences, including the vitiating of his
temper, and the loss of self-control. Yield larger things
to which you can show no more than equal right; and
yield lesser ones, though clearly your own. Better give
your path to a dog than be bitten by him in contesting
for the right. Even killing the dog would not cure the bite.*

ABRAHAM LINCOLN

I'm sure you've heard the comment, "You can dish it out, but you can't
take it." Well, there's more to effective conflict resolution than just
confronting others. What happens when confrontation is served in
your direction? When the shoe is on the other foot? When you're the
one being confronted? Do you have thin skin? Do you become angry?
Do you become critical? Do you feel threatened? Do you respond like
a martyr because you're being picked on? Do you rise up and attack?
Are you willing to change your behavior? Are you willing to develop
skills and grow your relationships skills?

When you're confronted or verbally attacked, your response is very
important. It's a good idea to plan ahead and be prepared. At some
point, everyone becomes the focus of some kind of confrontation. It's
part of the human experience. So here are some basics.

A Pre-Confrontation Guide

Do not respond immediately to the confrontation.

Take a deep breath and count to ten as you slowly let the air out. This will help to relax you and give you a brief moment to gather your thoughts. This is extremely important if you begin to feel angry.

Do not raise your voice. Speak softly and slowly. Measure your words deliberately.

Thank the confronters for their thoughts and feelings. Let them know their views are important to you and that you have heard their complaint.

Before you begin to deal with their complaint, ask, "Are there any other issues you would like to share with me?" This gives the confronters the opportunity to get everything off their chests. Sometimes the presenting complaint isn't the real issue. Often the confronters have the real or deeper issue waiting in the wings to be shared. The confronters may be "testing the water" to see how you will respond before they tell you what they really want to say. You may have to ask, "Is there anything else?" several times before the entire matter comes to the surface. Don't respond to the original complaint until you feel all the cards are on the table. Otherwise, you may find you've been set up for an even stronger confrontation.

POINT TO PONDER

It is nearly always better to discuss the problem in detail with your opponent before coming up with a proposed solution.

KENNETH CLOKE

As the confronters are talking with you, observe their body language and tonal quality, along with the verbal message. This will help you gauge the depth of their emotions and the strength of their convictions. Remember, you need all the information you can get before you respond.

Listen carefully to what their complaints and concerns are. Along the way, ask questions and seek clarification. This will help you keep your own emotions in control and clear up any misunderstandings.

Your listening and asking questions will also convey that you value them as people and their ideas are important to you. Sometimes people just need to be heard. You might ask, "When did you first begin to feel that way?" Or you might say, "What did I do to give you that impression?"

Be alert to your body language. What is your eye contact like? Do you find yourself looking away or directly at your confronters? Don't demonstrate your anger or frustration with frowns, sighs, or disagreeable looks. Your body language could escalate the problem.

Think about your role in the conflict. What have you done to contribute to the misunderstanding or disagreement?

POINT TO PONDER

Participants in conflict view themselves as innocent victims. They view the other person as the cause. Rarely do they see themselves as the cause or a key factor in the escalation of the conflict. It is difficult for them to acknowledge their role. Each person has a role in the conflict.

KENNETH CLOKE

Before you respond to accusations or complaints, rephrase and play back the complaint to the confronters. You might say, "Let me see if I've heard you correctly..." After you've relayed back their complaint, ask, "Have I accurately understood what you've shared with me?" Don't forget to keep silent after each question so they can respond. Even if there is a long pause, don't be afraid of silence. Give the confronters time to clear up any misunderstandings. The reframing of the issue helps to defuse anger and hostility. It also gives the confronters a graceful way to stay in the communication game and cooperate toward resolution. Remember, part of conflict resolution is a training process for everyone involved. How you treat others will model and train them how to treat you and others during conflicts.

Keep in mind that some people do not play fair. They may stay in confront mode. They may attempt to change the subject to more negatives. They may confuse the issues by discussing other problematic matters and minor details. Some people want to throw up all their anger and "barf out" all their hostility. They have no thought or desire for resolution. These individuals may be wrapped up in anger, rigidity, and intolerance. They may be dealing with fear, paranoia, or some emotional impairment.

In these cases you may have to stop talking about the issues and talk about the process of what is going on. Their dirty tricks and unproductive presentation may need to be exposed for what it is. Hopefully, when the light of truth comes on their method of dealing with issues, their behaviors will modify. But that's not always the case. You could be rejected. The only thing you can do is be open, honest, and firm. This is part of the risk-taking involved in conflict management.

POINT TO PONDER

It is far more difficult to collaborate during conflict because it takes strength to become vulnerable and move toward your opponent when that person is attacking you.

KENNETH CLOKE

Ask the confronters what they would like to see changed. How would they like the matter resolved? Find out what the other person wants. Attempting to resolve the issue before you know all the variables would be foolish. Only when you know their goals can you say you understand their complaint and concerns—and whether you will accept part or all of what they say or want...or that your answer is no because you are in complete disagreement with them.

After you get all the information, you're ready to respond. You will have your emotions under control. You've given yourself time to think through the issue and clarify points if needed. You have determined how important this issue is to everyone involved. You are in a position to more effectively resolve the conflict.

Peg Pickering, in her book *How to Manage Conflict*, suggests what is called the "ACES" approach to conflict:

A *Assess* the situation.

C *Clarify* the issues.

E *Evaluate* alternative approaches.

S *Solve* the problem.

This approach can certainly be used when you're the one being confronted. Take time to truly assess the situation. Once you have done that, you can clarify the issues and evaluate the alternative approaches. Then you'll be in a position to offer potential solutions to the problem. Learning to accept conflicts and handle confrontation with wisdom and grace is a lifelong learning process. As you continue to learn and grow, you'll witness some positive changes in your life when it comes to conflict resolution and relationships.

THE SERENITY PRAYER

God, grant me the Serenity
To accept the things I cannot change...
Courage to change the things I can;
And Wisdom to know the difference.

Living one day at a time,
Enjoying one moment at a time,
Accepting hardship as the pathway to peace.
Taking, as He did, this sinful world as it is,
Not as I would have it.

Trusting that He will make all things right
If I surrender to His Will.
That I may be reasonably happy in this life,
And supremely happy with Him
Forever in the next. Amen.

REINHOLD NIEBUHR

17

When You're Confronted About Someone Else

If we all told what we know of one another,
there would not be four friends in the world.

BLAISE PASCAL

What do you do when someone comes to you and wants to vent about someone else? Do you feel like you're being asked to take sides? What if you are friends with both people? How do you prevent yourself from getting sucked in to the conflict? One of the most helpful-yet-least-used concepts in dealing with difficult people is recognizing the theory of "Triangling." This concept was developed by family counselor Murray Bowen, MD, in the 1950s.

Dr. Bowen suggested that the smallest form of society consists of two people. If these two people each have a good self-image and a healthy working relationship with each other, there is harmony. What happens when one or both do not have a good self-image or a healthy working relationship with each other? There is frustration, tension, and disharmony. This disharmony can lead to arguments, fights, and separation. In some cases, it can lead to death, which is a permanent cutting off of relationship.

In the process of counseling families, Dr. Bowen noticed that families of origin develop "triangles." These triangles are formed when there is disharmony between two of the family members. The individual who feels tension mounting and emotional disharmony to the greatest degree will invariably "triangle" or involve a third party. A triangle is the smallest stable social relationship.

For example, let's say a husband and wife are having marital difficulties. The wife might feel the most emotionally disturbed about the disharmony in the marriage. As a result, she might triangle a close friend by venting her frustrations and pouring her energies into that particular relationship. This triangling helps the wife take her focus off the problems with her husband and put her energy into someone else. The result is that the marriage is temporarily stabilized even if the marital problems aren't resolved. The person who feels the most tension needs to vent tension.

Of course, the most ideal thing would be for the husband and wife to resolve the conflict between them. But, alas, this is not always done. Sometimes it seems easier to talk to others about our problems than personally face the annoying people in our lives. Why do you think this is the case?

POINT TO PONDER

If you find yourself unable to think of anything positive to say about your opponent, you are probably not yet emotionally ready for closure. Indeed, this is a good test to determine how far you have come in ending your conflict.

KENNETH CLOKE

Let's illustrate this concept further. Let's suppose that party "A" and party "B" have a relationship with each other. They may be married. They may be a child and a parent. They might be coworkers. They could be boss and employee or police and speeder. I'm sure you get the idea. Then a conflict comes between them.

Let's say party "A" feels the most discomfort and tension in the relationship. Because of this tension, party A will triangle with a third party...party "C."

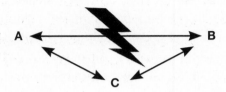

Party "C" has some form of relationship with parties "A" and "B." Party "A" unloads frustrations about party "B" into the ears of party "C." This may be in the form of storytelling or gossip. It could be under the guise of needing advice. It might even be as a warning to party "C" to watch out for party "B."

In any case, the more party "A" complains, the better party "A" feels. Party "A" has released tension, shared anger and resentment, and maybe even gotten back at party "B" a bit. The more party "C" listens and agrees with party "A," the closer the two are drawn together. The closer they become, the further they push party "B" away.

This type of triangling happens all the time. In fact, I would be willing to guess that you'll be triangled in some form this very week. It might be at home, at work, at church, or another type of social gathering. Triangling happens so often that we often to fail to recognize it for what it is. Triangles are almost automatic and require very little intellectual awareness.

Let's go even further. If the tension is great enough, party "A" may not be satisfied with just talking to party "C." Party "A" might want to get more people involved, to build a coalition against party "B." Party "A" may develop a complex network or series of three-person relationship systems. This development of small triangles might be done openly, such as a rally of some type, or covertly at the office water fountain, during coffee breaks, over lunch, or at social gatherings. The mainstay for triangling is usually gossip or storytelling. It's a situation where the "understanding ones" get together and talk about those who aren't present to defend themselves.

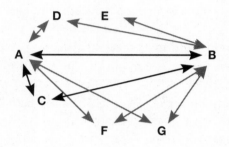

Most triangling causes more disharmony by generating more hurt feelings. It creates dissension and causes friends, relatives, and coworkers to choose sides. Often triangling is used as a form of manipulation. It's a socially accepted method of talking against people, such as bosses, teachers, ministers, relatives, and close family members.

Have you been triangled? Have you been sucked into a whirlpool of hostility before you could swim away? Have you been hurt by people in your life who roped you in to their troubles? Have you triangled others and shared your bitterness and anger with them? Have you been the instigator of hurt?

You see, *everyone* has played a role in triangling. It's a fact of life... part of the human experience. However, it is possible to lessen the negative effects of this powerful social tool.

POINT TO PONDER

Start with the assumption that all resistance reflects an unmet need.

KENNETH CLOKE

The first step is to develop an awareness of triangling. This requires controlling your spoken words. It involves developing emotional objectivity. It means growing in emotional maturity. The more alert you are to triangling, the less power it will have over you.

Avoiding the Trap of Triangling

Don't allow yourself to get sucked into gossip.

POINT TO PONDER

I am more deadly than the screaming shell from the howitzer. I win without killing. I tear down homes, break hearts, and wreck lives. I travel on the wings of the wind. No innocence is strong enough to intimidate me, no purity pure enough to daunt me. I have no regard for truth, no respect for justice, no mercy for the defenseless. My victims are as numerous as the sands of the sea, and often as innocent. I never forget and seldom forgive. My name is Gossip.

MORGAN BLAKE

Don't let your emotions run away with the information handed you. Stay calm and search for truth.

Don't be forced to choose sides. Strive to remain untriangled. This is done by objective observation. Look at the seriousness of the situation and balance it with the humor of the situation. If you are party "C," try to keep a healthy emotional distance. Remember that problems between party "A" and party "B" will resolve themselves if the parties keep in contact and, possibly, ask an objective third party to assist them. Encourage the parties to talk it out. Don't take no for an answer. Maintain meaningful emotional contact without becoming over involved.

Don't accept defeat. Keep in mind that if you can help resolve or modify the conflict in the central triangle, the other networks of small triangles will probably also get resolved. They often feed off the first triangle's basic problem. King Solomon wrote, "Throw out the mocker, and you will be rid of tension, fighting, and quarrels" (Proverbs 22:10).

Don't forget the importance of person-to-person relationships. Help others and yourself remember to talk *to* people instead of *about* people.

POINT TO PONDER

Conflict camouflages our weaknesses and diverts attention from sensitive subjects we would rather avoid discussing. It is a smokescreen, a way of passing the buck, blaming others, and distracting attention from our mistakes.

KENNETH CLOKE

18

Conflict Resolution for the Brave and Courageous

God grant me the courage not to give up what I think is right, even though I think it is hopeless.

CHESTER W. NIMITZ

I'm ready to quit!" said Colson as he sank into a chair in my office. His face looked more sad and hurt than angry.

"What's going on?" I asked.

"I found out there's a strong rumor that I'm getting the blame for something I didn't do."

"What are you being accused of?"

"Well, the event occurred about five years ago. The company bought a large and expensive stamping machine for the metal fabrication we do. After about seven months, it broke down and had to be replaced."

"What does that have to do with you?"

"Nothing! That's the point. This last week I was talking with my boss about a possible promotion to a new position. My present boss replaced the general manager and has been in the job for about four months. I asked him if I could be considered for a promotion. He said he didn't think so because of the breakdown of the stamping machine. I was taken aback. I asked him what he was talking about. He said he didn't think my judgment could be trusted because of the purchase and installation of that machine. The reason it broke down was because I bought the wrong machine for the job and, on top of that, I installed it wrong."

"That sounds pretty serious."

"Yeah, especially since it's not true. I was part of a committee that discussed the need for the new stamping machine and that's all. I didn't purchase it, and I didn't install it."

"Did you tell him that?"

"Yes, but it was evident he didn't believe me. He told me that the previous general manager had mentioned the problem to him. Now I'm not being considered for the new position. It's not right. It's so untrue and unfair. My reputation has been destroyed for something that happened five years ago that I didn't even do!"

In chapter 4, we looked at the physical effects caused by the stress of conflict. In chapter 5, we touched on the mental and emotional aspects of conflict. In this chapter, we'll look a little deeper into the emotional side of conflict and explore six major principles in conflict resolution.

I'm sure you've heard the familiar saying that in real estate the three most important things are location, location, location. Similarly, the three most important things in conflict are perception, perception, perception. Our perceptions determine our emotions. For the general manager in the story, it was the *perception* (right or wrong) that Colson's judgment and actions couldn't be trusted that was the critical factor. For Colson, his perception was that his reputation was destroyed. Both Colson and the general manager had appropriate emotions triggered by their perceptions.

The following flowchart gives a fairly typical response for most conflict situations. The depth of emotions encountered depend on the severity of the hurt that's felt or the loss that has been experienced. In Colson's case, he would most likely experience deeper emotions because hurt and loss were greater for him than for his boss, who had only been in the position for four months.

Conflict can be likened to dominos lined up in a row. As you push one domino over it hits the next domino…and so on until the whole row responds and all are knocked down. Emotions are similar. It starts with some kind of relationship. It could be a real relationship or an assumed relationship.

Then some type of conflict or disagreement occurs that sets off a domino of emotions. Within all conflicts is some type of hurt or loss.

TYPICAL CONFLICT RESPONSE FLOWCHART

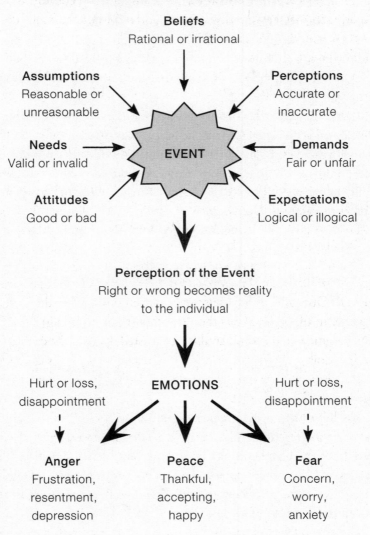

Beliefs
Rational or irrational

Assumptions
Reasonable or
unreasonable

Perceptions
Accurate or
inaccurate

Needs
Valid or invalid

EVENT

Demands
Fair or unfair

Attitudes
Good or bad

Expectations
Logical or illogical

Perception of the Event
Right or wrong becomes reality
to the individual

Hurt or loss,
disappointment

EMOTIONS

Hurt or loss,
disappointment

Anger
Frustration,
resentment,
depression

Peace
Thankful,
accepting,
happy

Fear
Concern,
worry,
anxiety

When someone hurts us or we lose finances, position, reputation, or relationship, one of the first emotions we feel is disappointment.

The disappointment can be compounded by anger (at what was done or not done) or fear that the relationship may be damaged. The situation can be further intensified by the desire to get even and have some type of revenge. That can be accomplished through gossip, unkind words, damaging a reputation, and so forth.

I'm reminded of two friends who were talking together. One friend said to the other, "I don't like to criticize, so I've made a decision to never say anything about someone unless it's good...and boy is this dirt good!"

Criticism likes to lay blame on someone else's shoulders. The goal of personal criticism is to make other people feel shame for the way they've treated you. The offended individual builds in faulty or distorted information in conversations designed to cause hurt. Rigidity and faulty assumptions are the fuel of criticism. Personal criticism is usually an attempt to hurt someone.

Psychologists tell us there are three common reasons people criticize others:

- We criticize the very thing we are guilty of or what tempts and troubles us the most.

- We criticize to project our own miserableness and our desire for others to join us.

- We criticize to elevate ourselves and to put others down and in their place.

If the problem or conflict isn't resolved, it can lead to frustration and defensive reactions. We may have the desire to withdraw (moving away from the people physically or emotionally). We may decide to attack (try to hurt them or put them down). We might try and resolve the conflict through compromise (which doesn't really deal with the issue at hand or resolve it).

The turmoil we feel inside over the damaged relationship may give rise to anxiety and depression. When we are hurt long enough by people or the loss has been great, we develop a lack of trust toward that individual or group. ("How could they do this? It's not right!") As trust ebbs, loss of respect grows. As loss of respect increases, resentment sprouts. Bitterness develops toward them and what they did. In the end, hatred and malice take root. Not a pretty picture.

EMOTIONAL DOMINOES

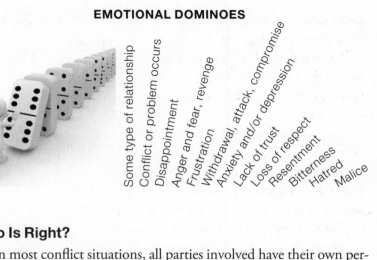

Who Is Right?

In most conflict situations, all parties involved have their own perceptions about the situation. Each party believes they're right and the others are wrong. How does that happen?

In all conflicts there are facts, details, and behaviors that take place. As each of the parties involved reflects on the details, they begin to develop "their story" regarding what happened and why their perceptions are accurate. They choose certain facts, behaviors, and details that best present their case.

For conflict resolution to take place, it's essential that all parties be willing to listen to the others and understand how they came to their conclusions. What hampers resolution is that each party has a tendency to judge the motivation or lack thereof behind the other people's behavior.

POINT TO PONDER

Rather than claim our experience to be The Truth, we need to understand that our experience, while certainly true for us, is not necessarily true for anyone else, especially for our opponents.

KENNETH CLOKE

CONFLICT SITUATION: FACTS, DETAILS, BEHAVIORS

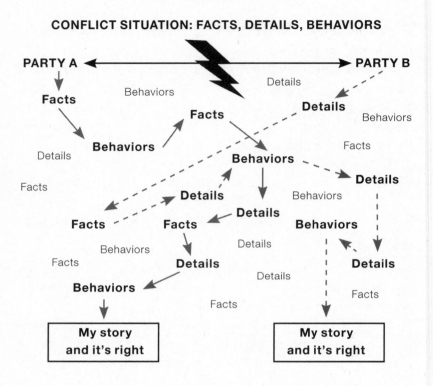

The problem lies in the fact that people don't really know the motivation of other people. All we see is their behavior. Then we make the mistake of *assuming* we know their intentions. Solomon, the wisest king mentioned in the Old Testament, addressed this when he said, "He who gives an answer before he hears, it is folly and shame to him" (Proverbs 18:13 NASB).

We often know our own motivation and intention. That's why we think we're right in our beliefs and actions. And since we don't know the motivations and intentions of others, we decide they must be wrong since they disagree with us.

This brings to mind the story of the father and his son who were riding on a train. For a period of time the father was deep in thought and staring out the window. The little boy, who was about four years of age, was wandering all over the train car. He ran up and down the aisle and made noise. He climbed on vacant seats and talked to people. He bounced up and down on the seats.

Finally a woman could no longer sit quietly and tolerate the boy's unruly behavior. She got up and went over to the father. "You should be ashamed of yourself," said the woman. "You're just sitting here ignoring the misbehavior of your boy. What are you going to do about the way he's behaving?"

The father was obviously startled by the strong words of the woman. "Oh, I'm terribly sorry. I was deep in thought…thinking about my wife. She died in an automobile accident two days ago. Her body is in the baggage car. We're taking her back home to be buried. I'll take care of my son right away."

Immediately the woman's attitude changed as compassion filled her heart. When the people in the car understood the circumstances surrounding the father and son, their sympathy was aroused and their patience increased.

Conflict usually contains an accusation of some kind. "You have done something to me" or "You have not done something for me." But there's often a deeper level that's unspoken…a hidden confession. The offending party often isn't told about this or why that reason is so

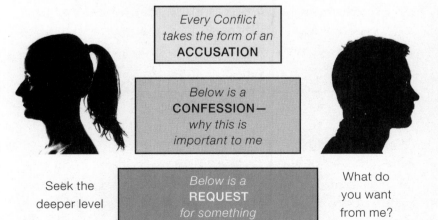

CONFLICT

Every Conflict takes the form of an **ACCUSATION**

Below is a **CONFESSION—** *why this is important to me*

Seek the deeper level

Below is a **REQUEST** *for something*

What do you want from me?

important. Neither is the unspoken request that goes along with that need. We really want the people to behave differently toward us, but we have a hard time telling them what we would like to see changed in the relationship.

Six Principles for Dispute Resolution

Dr. Kenneth Cloke, founder of the Center for Dispute Resolution, suggests there are six major principles in conflict resolution.

Physical Calming—Stop the Fighting—De-escalation
Separation, Reduce Stress, Give Time

If two young boys were fighting in the schoolyard, what's the first thing that needs to be done? Simple. The boys need to be separated and given some time to cool down. The same is true for adults. During conflict, they need to separate and take time to cool down and think through the issue. Then they can talk with each other and hopefully come to an acceptable resolution. If they fail to settle the issue, the conflict will remain in some form.

POINT TO PONDER

While adversarial conflicts can produce beneficial outcomes, they can also result in alienation, defensiveness, counterattack, and resistance. Worse, they can create a quality of energy and attitude that gives an appearance of strength while actually sapping it.

KENNETH CLOKE

Mental Calming—Settle the Issues—Ending
Analysis, Clarification, Compromise

Often a mediator, negotiator, arbitrator, referee, consultant, or some type of facilitator can be beneficial. A conciliator helps the parties talk with each other, express their concerns and desires, and reach some form of mutual understanding and agreement. However, it's possible that surface conflict issues can be settled but the underlying reasons are left unsettled. If that occurs, the conflict will go underground and reappear in the future.

POINT TO PONDER

In conflicts, trust is broken, cruel words are spoken, friendships dissolve, love turns into hate, and hate into revenge. The simplicity of this description belies the complexity of its experience.

KENNETH CLOKE

Emotional Calming—Resolving Underlying Reasons— Completion | Listening, Acceptance, Dialogue

With the help of a mediator, the issues could be settled and the underlying reasons behind the conflict may be addressed. In the case of the two boys in the schoolyard, separation and fighting can be stopped. The reason for the fighting, which might be bullying or name calling, might cease. However, if the two boys haven't forgiven each other and made friends, the conflict can be trapped in a cycle of unforgiveness.

POINT TO PONDER

Intellectual techniques may be highly effective in settling disputes but less likely to resolve the underlying emotional issues in the conflict. Emotional techniques may be successful in resolving the underlying issues, but less likely to encourage forgiveness. To reach forgiveness, spiritual techniques are required. To achieve reconciliation, it is necessary for people to open their hearts, explore what triggered the conflict internally within them, reconnect with their opponents, and transcend the reasons that gave rise to their conflict.

KENNETH CLOKE

Spiritual Calming—Reaching Forgiveness—Closure
Forgiveness, Insight, Reconciliation

Forgiveness is a difficult task. In the next chapter we'll address why forgiveness can be so difficult in greater detail. For now, understand that it's possible to forgive someone for what he or she has done and yet not be reconciled. For example, you may have had an abusive parent who hurt you physically and emotionally. As you grew older, you may have come to the place where you forgave that parent for the way you were treated. That's good and healthy, but it doesn't mean you reconciled. He or she may have died before you forgave. Or the parent may be alive but have no desire to have anything to do with you. In that case, the fragments of conflict still remain. If you're not careful, those fragments can create stress, illness, divorce, job conflicts, and bitterness.

POINT TO PONDER

Even if people feel ready, willing, and able to open their hearts to each other, it is not easy to become reconciled with a former opponent after participating in adversarial conflict. This is partly because reconciliation requires trust, which resolution and forgiveness do not, and it is difficult to repair trust after it has been broken. Nonetheless, it is possible for former adversaries to gradually rebuild trust.

KENNETH CLOKE

"Heart-full" Calming—Making Reconciliation—Disappearance
Attitude, Vulnerability, Trust

The word "reconciled" means "to become friends again" or "to bring back harmony." When my brother and I were younger, we used to fight a lot with each other. When that would happen, my mother would punish us with the worst punishment we knew. She would not spank us. She would not wash our mouths out with soap. She would not use a switch on us. It was far worse than that. She would make my brother and me "kiss and make up." *Yuck!* I'd rather have a spanking than kiss my brother! However, it did work. We ended up laughing when we had to kiss each other. It brought back harmony and reconciliation... for a while at least.

Forgiveness	Reconciliation
A one-way street	A two-way street
Takes one person	Takes two people
Gives release	Attempts to rejoin
A change of thinking	A change of behaving
A free gift	An earned trust
Offered to offender	Offered to each other
Unconditional	Found in repentance
Resiliency	Humbleness

It's possible to reach forgiveness and even make reconciliation and still not take the next step. And what is that next step? To address the system, context, culture, and environment that helps to create conflict.

POINT TO PONDER

In its simplest form, forgiveness is a willingness to let the conflict go and release ourselves from the burden of our own false expectations.

KENNETH CLOKE

HOW TO APPROACH CONFLICT

Physical calming — de-escalation
(separate, reduce stress, give time)

Mental calming — ending
(analysis, clarification, compromise)

Emotional calming — completion
(listening, acceptance, dialogue)

Spiritual calming — closure
(forgiveness, insight, reconciliation)

"Heart-full" calming — prevention
(tradition, morale, instruction)

Cultural Calming — Design Preventative Systems — Prevention
Tradition, Morale, Instruction

This involves structures, cultures, and environments that make it more difficult for future conflict. It involves education on listening skills, choosing your words carefully, observing body language, developing confrontation skills, and improving communication techniques. Conflict resolution abilities begin in the home and need to be modeled by parents. Schools, businesses, and other institutions have a responsibility to develop healthy conflict resolution programs.

POINT TO PONDER

At the center or heart of every conflict lies a pathway to resolution, forgiveness, and reconciliation.

KENNETH CLOKE

Blessed are the peacemakers,
for they will be called children of God.

MATTHEW 5:9 NIV

19

Why Is Forgiveness So Difficult?

Everyone says forgiveness is a lovely idea,
until they have something to forgive.

C.S. LEWIS

As Karen approached, I could tell something was wrong. She didn't have her typical smile and lighthearted spirit.

"Bob, do you have a moment to talk?"

"Sure. What's up?"

"Well...um..."

I could see Karen was choosing her words carefully.

"I'm really confused...I'm deeply hurt...I'm really struggling."

She went on to share her story. The church she was attending had a desire to reach out to homeless mothers with children. These were women who were in abusive situations and needed assistance. A number of deacons, along with the pastor, had asked her if she would be willing to help by taking up the leadership of the outreach.

Karen agreed. With great enthusiasm, she spent the next nine months organizing volunteers to join her. Through their combined efforts, they were able to raise enough money to purchase a home, which they remodeled for the mothers with children. Karen was instrumental in contacting a foundation that donated a large amount of funding toward the project.

Everything was going fine until one day the pastor approached her. He informed her that he wanted another woman in the church to assist her. Being a little overworked, the idea of assistance sounded helpful.

It wasn't long after that when she noticed that the assistant seemed to be taking on more responsibilities and making decisions that Karen usually made.

She wrote several e-mails to the pastor asking for clarification of her role and the role of her assistant. The responses she received from the pastor were confusing and didn't really address the issues. It wasn't long after that when the pastor called and informed her that he wanted her assistant to take over the homeless mother's program.

Karen was shocked. She wrote a couple of other e-mails to the pastor trying to understand what was going on and why the sudden change. What she received was silence. No response. Even some of the deacons who had originally encouraged her were withdrawing in silence.

Then one day Karen received a text from the pastor asking her to not approach the foundation about asking for any further funds. He informed her that he would be doing that. Now, she was really confused. Had she done something wrong? What was going on?

Over the next couple of weeks, she began hearing secondhand reports that some of the deacons thought she had been dishonest. When she attempted to get clarification, she was ignored. She felt like her reputation was being destroyed.

"I'm trying to take the higher road and be the bigger person, but it's hard. I've tried to find out what I did so I can fix the situation, but neither the pastor nor the deacons will discuss it. What should I do?"

Hurt and loss are common in this life. No relationships are without tension at some point. We can't live in a community of people without experiencing conflicts. In fact, in any human relationship there's the possibility of pain, injury, suffering, and alienation.

And all of us tend to assign blame to the other person or event for our troubles. When we're hurt by others, whether they yell or are silent, we avoid them. Sometimes we pretend the problem doesn't exist, reverting to denial. Often we resent those who have done us wrong. An old adage says, "If the other person injures you, you may forget the injury; but if you injure him, you will always remember." Jane Porter suggests, "The best manner of avenging ourselves is by not resembling him who has injured us."

Resentment comes from the accumulation of unexpressed anger and is one of the most destructive emotions in human relationships. It can destroy personal well-being and emotional health. The definition of "resentment" comes from the concept "to feel strongly." Resentment seems to give us power and control of others. We can use this emotion to avoid communication with those whom we do not like. We can use it like a shield to protect us from being hurt again. Resentment can make others feel guilty for hurting us. It helps us avoid our true feelings about the hurtful event. Resentment justifies our "victim" status and helps us keep believing we're correct in our view of the matter. It can short-circuit our taking responsibility for our thoughts and behaviors. Resentment can develop into a deep grudge and extreme bitterness.

Unfortunately, being resentful is like biting a dog after it has bitten you. It eventually becomes an executioner. It destroys us instead of the person we're mad at. Resentment becomes self-inflicted torture.

Dealing with Hurt

Let's take a minute and look at hurt. There are basically two types. One is "fair" hurt and the other is "unfair" hurt.

Fair Hurt

An example of fair hurt would be losing a bet. If I bet $50 on a horse in a race, and it lost, losing my bet would be fair. No one made me place the bet. I did it on my own accord. I have to take responsibility for the decision. If I light a firecracker and hold it in my hand while it goes off, I will be hurt. That's a cause-and-effect hurt. If I don't study for a test and fail, it will hurt my grade point average. That comes under the category of "what I sow I will also reap," which is also a fair hurt. If I tell my boss off and I get fired, that's fair because my boss had reasonable grounds to let me go. Most "fair" hurt is when the person we should get angry with is ourselves. There's very little help for foolishness or stupidity.

Unfair Hurt

If I lose $50 because a thief mugs me on the street, that's unfair hurt. If a drunk driver drives into my car and kills one of my family members, that's definitely unfair hurt. If some pyromaniac starts a fire in a house next to mine, and the fire spreads to my house, that's unfair hurt. There are many hurts that come from "outside forces." In some cases, unfair hurt is from the *perception* of a situation. For example, someone may make a comment as a joke, but I might perceive it as an attack or personal insult. "Let's play donkey. I'll be the head, and you be yourself." At this point, what makes it unfair to me is the "intent" behind the comment. Since no one can ever be sure of the intent or motivation of others, misunderstandings and miscommunications are always possible.

When it comes to forgiveness, there are some things people don't forgive. Forgiveness just doesn't apply in some situations:

1. *We don't forgive acts of nature.* When a tornado strikes our house, we don't forgive the tornado. We don't forgive a flood that sweeps across our property. Those are definitely forms of hurt, but we don't spend time forgiving acts of nature.

2. *We don't forgive systems.* When we experience driving too fast and get a ticket, we don't forgive the laws that were established. We don't forgive the Internal Revenue Service for our high taxes. We don't forgive schools for making us listen to boring teachers.

3. *We don't forgive those who have not hurt us.* If a car drives through a red light and hits our car, we don't forgive bystanders who saw the incident. They had nothing to do with it. When a friend tells us off in public, we don't forgive strangers who overhear the conversation.

4. *We only forgive people who have hurt us in some way.* People who hurt us can be divided into four categories.

   - *Some people want to hurt us.* They want to get even and make us feel bad.

   - *Some people hurt us as a spillover.* They've been hurt by others in some way and are letting their anger and frustration out on us.

   - *Some people hurt us with good intentions.* They might tell us we have bad breath or need deodorant.

   - *Some people are not aware they're hurting us.* There may be a suggested business proposal and not everyone in the organization agrees with it. They may make negative comments about an article without knowing we were the author of it.

There are some hurts that seem to be harder to get over. If I break your favorite dish, that's not the same depth of hurt as running over your dog. There are many hurts in life, but I believe there are four hurts that are very difficult to bear.

- *Disloyalty*—Breaking trust
- *Betrayal*—Being "stabbed in the back"
- *Brutality*—Physical, mental, and emotional violence
- *Shunning*—ignoring, treated like we don't exist

"Hurt is a stubborn stain in the fabric of our memory." There's no question that hurt and pain are inevitable. But we must be reminded that *suffering is optional.* You may have heard someone say, "If you haven't forgotten an offense toward you, you haven't truly forgiven it." That sounds very noble, but it's a lie. We don't forget painful events even if we've forgiven the individuals involved. "Forgiveness is not 'holy amnesia' that erases the past." Instead, it's the experience of healing that draws the poison out. Forgiveness simply removes the sting in the hornet of memory. Forgiveness allows us to recall the hurtful event without having to relive the hurt again.

I remember a childhood event in which a salesman in a variety store kicked me out of the store. I don't remember why he did it. I was probably horsing around, and he was justified in doing it. What I do remember is that I was very angry with him. I said to myself, "I'll not enter that store as long as he works there." My resentment grew, and I didn't go into that store for seven years. No big deal, right? Wrong. It was a big deal to a little boy because this was also the only candy store in the neighborhood. Who suffered the most by all my anger and resentment? Certainly not the salesperson. I'm reminded of the old saying, "Don't carry a grudge. While you're carrying the grudge, the other guy's out dancing."

If you've ever wondered why forgiveness is so difficult, remember that the injured party lets the person who has done the injury go free. Archibald Hart put it this way: "Forgiveness is surrendering my right to hurt you back if you hurt me." Mark Twain expressed the same concept when he stated, "Forgiveness is the fragrance the violet sheds on the heel that has crushed it."

Let's say that I came over to your house to visit. You invite me in, and we go into your living room. You say, "Please sit down." For some reason, I choose not to sit in a big, soft chair but instead sit down in a small rocking chair. Before you can speak, the small rocking chair collapses under my weight. You see, I didn't know it was an antique rocking chair that had been handed down through your family. To you, it was a "display" piece. Everyone is in shock that it's broken.

I say, "I'm sorry. Can I buy you another one?"

"No," you reply.

"Can I replace it?"

"No," you say with sadness and pain in your voice.

"Will you forgive me?"

Inside, you groan with pain.

Can you see why forgiveness is so difficult? The person who inflicts the injury goes free, leaving the injured party in pain and misery. This is a dirty deal. It's not fair. It's not a pleasant experience in the least.

Repayment for the offense is impossible. I can't put the broken chair back into the same condition it was before the accident. If you choose revenge, it will not replace the chair. Resenting me for breaking the chair will not restore it. In forgiveness, the injured party has to make peace with the pain and accept the loss. This is why most people don't like to forgive—it's too painful and too costly.

POINT TO PONDER

We need to surrender our search for emotional compensation for the wrongs that were done to us. What caused the conflict is now over, past, and done with. The only remaining question is whether we are willing to let go, solve the problems that led to it, and move on with our lives, or whether we would rather the conflict continue to cause us pain and be allowed to undermine our future.

KENNETH CLOKE

A Whale of a Story

You may recall the biblical story about Jonah, who was swallowed by a great fish. The story begins when Jonah is instructed by God to go to the city of Nineveh. He was given the task of crying out against the city because of its great wickedness (see the book of Jonah).

This assignment didn't sit well with Jonah. He didn't like the people of Nineveh. To put it bluntly, he hated them. He knew that God was a forgiving God and would forgive the people of Nineveh if they

FORGIVENESS ISN'T EASY

Legally
Forgiveness takes place when the injured party drops the charges, cancels the lawsuit for damages, and absorbs the loss incurred by the injurer.

Psychologically
Forgiveness takes place when the injured person who was offended and justly angered by the offender bears his own anger, and lets the other go free.

FORGIVENESS

Theologically
Forgiveness, whether human or divine, is essentially substitutional. It is vicarious. No man truly forgives his brother until he bears upon himself the hurt of the other's deed. God forgave us in Jesus because God was in Christ paying the cost of forgiving mankind by bearing the total hurt of our evil upon Himself at Calvary.

Practically
Forgiveness takes place when the person hurt, smeared, betrayed, or cheated, accepts the loss and pays the cost of forgiving the other's wrongs, asking for no repayment of the wrong, seeking no revenge to get back or even, and choosing to hold no resentment toward the offender.

would turn from their wickedness. Jonah didn't want to see them forgiven. He wanted to see them punished. He wanted them to pay for all the evil they had done.

The people of Nineveh were indeed cruel and wicked. They were known to skin their captives alive. They would cut out tongues, gouge out eyes, and mutilate bodies. They burned children alive and terrorized their enemies with a multitude of atrocities.

Because of his dislike of the assignment, Jonah tried to run away from it. He went in the opposite direction. He boarded a ship headed for the city of Tarshish, on the west end of the Mediterranean Sea. He was running away from what God wanted him to do.

While on the ocean, a mighty storm arose and threatened to destroy the ship and everyone on board. The sailors tried everything they could to keep the ship afloat. They eventually came to the conclusion that Jonah might be the cause of the storm. Jonah admitted that God had brought the storm, and that he was running away from Him. He told the sailors the storm would stop if they threw him into the sea.

It took some convincing, but the men threw Jonah overboard. Sure enough, the storm stopped. Jonah was swallowed by a great fish and remained in its belly for three days. During that time, God again reminded Jonah of his assignment to go to Nineveh and tell the people that in forty days the city would be overthrown and the people destroyed.

Jonah finally agreed and the fish threw him up on shore. Jonah went to the city and delivered God's message. The reluctant prophet left the city and went to a hill to wait and watch God destroy the city. He wanted to see those people get what they deserved.

To Jonah's dismay, the people heard his message. The whole city put on sackcloth and repented of their wicked ways. God forgave them for their past evil deeds. This caused Jonah to get very angry. He didn't think it was fair for those people to be given a free pass after all the hurt and conflict they'd caused. It made him so upset and depressed that he said, "It is better for me to die than to live" (Jonah 4:3 NIV).

Although centuries have passed since the days of Jonah, his attitude lingers on in people today. The desire to seek revenge and to get even with those who hurt us and others is still present. And even though God will forgive our enemies, we have a difficult time following His example.

For days Jonah sat and waited to see the destruction of the people of Nineveh, but it didn't come. A hot east wind came, and the sun beat down on his head. Jonah wished for death. He was angry with God. He didn't agree with what God was doing. The truism "When God and I don't agree about something, someone must be wrong" was certainly playing out.

When things don't go our way we feel the searing wind of anger. We want to throw a temper tantrum. The sun of bitterness and hatred beats down on our heads and fills our hearts. It causes pain and turmoil because we don't want to forgive others like God forgives us (Ephesians 4:32). We miss out on peace.

The story of Jonah abruptly ends with God saying to Jonah, "Is it right for you to be angry...?" Jonah responds by saying, "It is right for me to be angry enough to die!" Then the Lord said, "And why shouldn't I feel sorry for a great city like Nineveh?" (Jonah 4:9,11).

The story of Jonah and Nineveh is left open-ended. We don't know what Jonah finally did. We don't know if he forgave or if he died with bitterness raging in his heart. Your story is also open-ended. What are you going to do about your situation? Are you going to join in forgiveness or go to the grave with the weight of bitterness seething in your heart?

The Nuts and Bolts of Forgiveness

Forgiveness *is not* the denial of the emotions of hurt and anger. Forgiveness *does not* repress and hold down feelings. Forgiveness *does not* suppress the fullness of the pain. Forgiveness *does not* pretend that everything is fine and act nice when a problem exists. Forgiveness *is* very realistic. Forgiveness *is* honest; it *does not* hide its head in the sand, thinking that difficulties will go away if they're not acknowledged. Forgiveness *does not* fantasize that what is unchangeable can be changed or undone.

Forgiveness *does not* passively accept or condone unacceptable behavior. It *does not* rationalize, give alibis, or make excuses for the offending party. It doesn't mean being a doormat for evil to continue. Forgiveness *does not* equal tolerance. We can forgive almost anything... but we can't tolerate everything. Forgiveness *isn't* afraid to exercise tough love and tell the truth. Forgiveness *isn't* afraid to talk about repentance, restoration, and reconciliation. It's not an emotional umbilical cord that allows the offending party to avoid personal responsibility.

Forgiveness *is not* isolation from the person who has done the offending. It doesn't take on an attitude of superiority or piously hand out pity to the offender. Forgiveness *does not* place blame or make the other person feel guilty. Mahatma Gandhi said, "The weak can never forgive; forgiveness is the attribute of the strong."

Forgiveness is commanded by God in the Bible as an act of how we should live in harmony with others. Christ illustrated forgiveness when He died for our sins and let us go free:

> So, as those who have been chosen of God, holy and beloved, put on a heart of compassion, kindness, humility, gentleness and patience; bearing with one another, and forgiving each other, whoever has a complaint against anyone; just as the Lord forgave you, so also should you (Colossians 3:12-13 NASB).

This passage clarifies the attitude of those who forgive others. They have compassion. They look at the offending party with new eyes. They seek to understand the other person's motivation and background. They remember that the offender is precious in the eyes of God. Catherine the Great, "Empress of Russia," said, "The more a man knows, the more he forgives." Those who forgive are kind. They do not seek revenge; they seek restoration and reconciliation. Although they have been hurt, they try not to hurt back but ask, "How would Jesus respond in this situation?" Hannah More said, "A Christian will find it cheaper to pardon than to resent. Forgiveness saves the expense of anger, the cost of hatred, and the waste of spirits."

Those who forgive are humble. They try not to lord the offense over the offending party or make the person feel guilty. Those who forgive are gentle. They speak the truth in love with a desire to help offenders face their responsibility and grow through the experience. Being gentle and kind are acts of great courage and strength. *Being gentle is a choice.* St. Francis de Sales said, "Nothing is so strong as gentleness; nothing is so gentle as real strength."

Those who forgive are patient. Have you ever desired more patience? Patience comes from trouble. We don't need patience when everything is going our way—only when things are going against us do we need it. Those who forgive experience pain, hurt, and loss. They exercise patience toward the offending party, which increases patience overall. As people have said, "Patience is a bitter plant that has sweet fruit."

Those who forgive bear with one another. This entails more than putting up with others and their behaviors. It means "to carry the burden imposed by others without complaint." People who forgive let complaints roll off their backs. They endure the pain of the complaint and make the choice to deal with it and move on. This is illustrated in Proverbs 19:11 NIV: "A person's wisdom yields patience; it is to one's glory to overlook an offense."

The Limburger Cheese Syndrome

Sometimes it becomes very difficult to overlook an offense. We view the individual who has hurt us as an enemy. We see them as the cause of our heartache and conflict. In our thinking, they need to be punished in some way. We long to get revenge, to get even with them. We begin to view all of their behavior in a negative light. The more we think about them, the more we dislike them. The more we dislike them, the more they can do nothing right or good.

I'm reminded of the story of an uncle who came to visit his brother and family. After a large dinner, the uncle fell asleep on the couch. His brother's children decided to play a joke on the uncle. While he was asleep the children took some limburger cheese and lightly rubbed it on the large mustache of the uncle and then waited in anticipation for him to awake.

Finally he awoke, sat up, and sucked in a deep breath of air through his nose. He made a face and said, "It stinks in here!" He then walked into the dining room and said, "It stinks in here!" The children were giggling over their trick. The uncle walked on into the kitchen and said, "It stinks in here!" The children could hardly hold back their delight. The uncle then stepped outside and took a deep breath. He wrinkled his face and said, "The whole world stinks!" The children were now rolling on the grass with laughter.

Bitterness and resentment become like limburger cheese to us. Everything our enemy does stinks. Their words and actions smell to high heaven. Maybe we need to wash our noses and mustaches with the water of forgiveness.

Forgiveness doesn't come about by accident. It's a choice. It's an attitude. It's a process. It's a way of life. Forgiveness *is not* an emotion. If people had to wait until they *felt* like forgiving others, pigs would fly first. Forgiveness is found in the will. It's a promise. As Jay E. Adams suggests, it is a commitment to three things:

1. I will not use the event against them in the future.

2. I will not talk to others about them.

3. I will not dwell on it myself.

Forgiveness does not beat the offending party over the head with their offense, trying to make them feel bad. It does not try to destroy the reputation of the offending party or get revenge by sharing the transgression with others. Forgiveness does not wallow in the misery of the conflict. It gets up and moves on with life. It does not rip off the scabs to see if the offense is healing, for this only prolongs the hurt.

I had a friend who was speaking at a conference center during the summer. About halfway through the week, a woman came to him for counsel. She poured out the story of her divorce and the difficulty she was experiencing trying to get over it. After about twenty minutes, my friend said, "May I ask you a few questions?"

"Of course," said the woman.

"How long ago did your divorce occur?"

"About two years."

"How many people have you talked with this week about your divorce?"

"Including you?"

"Yes, including me."

The woman thought for a moment and said, "About six."

To which my friend responded, "You know, I think I too would have a hard time getting over my divorce if I talked to six people a week about it for two years."

Clara Barton, the founder of the American Red Cross, was once reminded of an especially cruel thing that had been done to her years before, but she seemed not to recall it. "Don't you remember it?" her friend asked. "No," came the reply. "I distinctly remember forgetting the incident." An adage worth knowing states, "There is no point in burying the hatchet if you're going to put up a marker on the site."

Forgiveness has the courage to work through problems rather than ignoring them or pretending they don't exist. Jesus addressed this:

> If your brother sins, go and show him his fault in private; if he listens to you, you have won your brother. But if he does not listen to you, take one or two more with you, so that *by the mouth of two or three witnesses every fact may be confirmed.* If he refuses to listen to them, tell it to the church; and if he refuses to listen even to the church, let him be to you as a Gentile and a tax collector (Matthew 18:15-17 NASB).

Which Comes First, the Chicken or the Egg?

What is the purpose of forgiveness? The act of forgiveness restores and attempts to reconcile broken relationships. What happens if one of the parties doesn't want to restore the relationship? Does forgiveness still take place? That is like asking, "Which comes first, the chicken or the egg?" Does forgiveness take place first and then repentance, or does repentance take place first and then forgiveness?

To answer the first question—the chicken comes first. God doesn't lay eggs. To answer the second question—forgiveness comes first and then repentance. Christ is our example of this. He forgives our sins *before* we repent. The joy that forgiveness brings comes when we repent and turn from our sin. We can forgive others their offenses, but we both may not experience the joy of restoration and reconciliation until repentance of the offender occurs. Sometimes they don't repent, and we are left with a true-but-hollow-feeling forgiveness. That's a painful experience.

When we forgive someone and they do not repent, we hurt. In a very small way, we experience how God feels when people won't turn from their sins and accept His forgiveness. The heart of God aches because of His love for them. He doesn't turn His back on them because of their rejection. He keeps reaching out with the desire that someday they will repent and run into His arms. We should follow His example.

What happens if the offenders hurt us again after we've forgiven them? Jesus addresses this when talking with Peter:

> Peter came and said to [Jesus], "Lord, how often shall my brother sin against me and I forgive him? Up to seven times?" Jesus said to him, "I do not say to you, up to seven times, but up to seventy times seven" (Matthew 18:21-22 NASB).

Dear reader, how many times has God forgiven your transgressions? I've been asked, "What if the person I need to forgive has moved out of town and I can't locate him? What if the person I need to forgive has died?" Then I suggest you do the same thing the Old Testament leaders did when they owed money to someone who died or moved away. They brought the money owed to the temple as an offering to God. They gave the obligation to the Lord. If you need to forgive someone who has passed away or can't be found, bring your forgiveness to the Lord as an offering.

You Did Me Wrong!

The classic story in the Bible about forgiveness is the story of Joseph. Joseph's brothers were extremely jealous of him. They plotted to murder him, but then they decided to sell him into slavery instead. They sold him, and eventually Joseph became a slave to a man called Potiphar. Joseph made the best of his unfortunate circumstance and worked very diligently. He did such a good job and proved his trustworthiness that Potiphar put him in charge of all the other house servants. Potiphar's wife was attracted to Joseph and tried to seduce him. Being a man of integrity, Joseph ran from the situation.

Potiphar's wife was angry at being rejected. She made up a story and told her husband that Joseph had attempted to rape her. After Potiphar had him thrown into prison, Joseph again endeavored to make the best of his situation. The warden of the prison eventually put Joseph in charge of the other prisoners.

While in prison, Joseph helped two prisoners, only asking that they endeavor to free him after they were released. The cupbearer of Pharaoh forgot about Joseph's request, and Joseph remained in prison for at least another two years. Eventually, the cupbearer remembered Joseph, and he was brought before Pharaoh. Through a set of circumstances, Joseph eventually became the second in command under the Pharaoh of Egypt!

Up to this point in Joseph's life, we've learned several things of importance. The first is that Joseph faced many difficulties and was hurt greatly by those around him:

1. His brothers were jealous of him and hated him.

2. He was sold into slavery.

3. Potiphar's wife made up stories about him and slandered his reputation.

4. Potiphar had him thrown into prison.

5. The cupbearer forgot about him, so Joseph spent more time in prison.

Joseph was treated unfairly. He lost his freedom, his reputation, his family. You'd think that these experiences would make him angry and bitter. You'd think he would long for revenge, to get even with the people who had deliberately hurt him. But he didn't.

Another thing we learned about Joseph was that he did not dwell on his misfortunes and wallow in his misery. He overcame his circumstances by being diligent in his work. He took all the lemons in his life and made lemonade. Few things are more effective than good, hard work for getting our minds off our troubles. One pardons to the degree that one loves.

The third thing we learn about Joseph is that he was a man filled with forgiveness. We see this when his brothers came to Egypt to buy food for their family. The brothers don't recognize Joseph, but Joseph recognized them. He now had the perfect opportunity to get even, but Joseph chooses, instead, to forgive.

This wonderful story is found in the book of Genesis, chapters 37 to 50. At one point in the story, Joseph reveals himself to his brothers:

> Then Joseph could no longer control himself before all his attendants, and he cried out, "Have everyone leave my

presence!" So there was no one with Joseph when he made himself known to his brothers. And he wept so loudly that the Egyptians heard him, and Pharaoh's household heard about it.

Joseph said to his brothers, "I am Joseph! Is my father still living?" But his brothers were not able to answer him, because they were terrified at his presence. Then Joseph said to his brothers, "Come close to me." When they had done so, he said, "I am your brother Joseph, the one you sold into Egypt! And now, do not be distressed and do not be angry with yourselves for selling me here, because it was to save lives that God sent me ahead of you. For two years now there has been famine in the land, and for the next five years there will not be plowing and reaping. But God sent me ahead of you to preserve for you a remnant on earth and to save your lives by a great deliverance. So then, it was not you who sent me here, but God" (Genesis 45:1-8)

The fourth quality we learn about Joseph was that he didn't make his brothers feel guilty for their ill treatment of him. He didn't demand any form of repayment for their offense.

Then we discover Joseph saw the big picture regarding the problems in his life. He knew God was in control, and that He was not surprised at all the difficulties Joseph had faced. Joseph realized God had something for him to learn from the pain and misery. He trusted God, and he believed that all the events in his life would eventually bring God glory. Joseph worked through his problems by faith.

The sixth thing we learn about Joseph was that he was very gracious, kind, and gentle. We see this when Joseph's father passes away. His brothers thought Joseph was just being nice because their father was living. Now that their father was dead, they feared Joseph would exercise his revenge and retaliate. That's what they would have done.

When Joseph's brothers saw that their father was dead, they said, "What if Joseph holds a grudge against us and pays us back for all the wrongs we did him?" So they sent word to

Joseph, saying, "Your father left these instructions before
he died: 'This is what you are to say to Joseph: I ask you to
forgive your brothers the sins and the wrongs they committed in treating you so badly.' Now please forgive the sins of
the servants of the God of your father." When their message came to him, Joseph wept.

His brothers then came and threw themselves down before him.
"We are your slaves," they said. But Joseph said to them, "Don't be
afraid. Am I in the place of God? You intended to harm me, but God
intended it for good to accomplish what is now being done, the saving
of many lives. So then, don't be afraid. I will provide for you and your
children." And he reassured them and spoke kindly to them (Genesis 50:15-21).

Dear reader, please reread the life of Joseph and ask yourself, "What
lessons does God want to teach me through the life of Joseph?" My
prayer for you is that you may realize that the difficult situations you
face and the harm brought on by others can be used by God to help
you grow and influence the lives of others for Him.

Praise be to the God and Father of our Lord Jesus Christ,
the Father of compassion and the God of all comfort, who
comforts us in all our troubles, so that we can comfort
those in any trouble with the comfort we ourselves receive
from God. For just as we share abundantly in the sufferings of Christ, so also our comfort abounds through Christ.
If we are distressed, it is for your comfort and salvation; if
we are comforted, it is for your comfort, which produces
in you patient endurance of the same sufferings we suffer.
And our hope for you is firm, because we know that just as
you share in our sufferings, so also you share in our comfort (2 Corinthians 1:3-7).

POINT TO PONDER

Sometimes we find it hard to forgive. We forget that forgiveness is as much for us as for the other person. If you can't forgive it's like holding a hot coal in your hand—you're the one getting burned.

JENNIFER JAMES

Dear God,

You're going to have to help me, please. I've been carrying hurt and anger so long that I don't have the strength to lift it off my back. I've been wallowing in the muddy swamp of resentment, and I don't know how to climb out. I've tried, but I keep sliding back in.

Please send a rescue team immediately! Also send a big water truck of forgiveness to wash away the pain and self-pity that has covered my life. I would like to get cleaned up so I can be used by You to help others who are in the swamp. Amen.

Closing Thoughts

Pity the human being who is not able to connect faith within himself with the infinite...He who has faith has...an inward reservoir of courage, hope, confidence, calmness, and assuring trust that all will come out well—even though the world...may appear to come out most badly.

B.C. FORBES

Conflict is a universal human experience. It can manifest itself in small issues, such as someone driving too close to your bumper on the freeway. It can also be experienced in large issues that affect your entire family. No single book can cover all the necessary information for conflict resolution. *Overcoming Conflict* was written to help you take a new look at the subject. It's my prayer that the material presented has provoked thought and offered new tools that will lead you to positive action in conflict reduction and resolution.

Conflict is like the common cold. It's here to stay. It affects us physically, mentally, emotionally, and spiritually. At some point we need to ask ourselves, "Do we want to be part of the problem or part of the solution?" We would be wise to consider these three questions when conflict raises its ugly head:

1. What is going on?
2. How do I feel about it?
3. Do I want to change the situation?

My experience as a counselor has revealed that people generally change only when they hurt enough. Until that time, they will continue to behave in a manner that gives them some kind of reward or satisfaction—whether their behavior is negative or positive.

James MacDonald shares a story in his book *I Really Want to Change...So, Help Me, God* along this line. It's the story of Raynald, who was a fourteenth-century duke in Belgium. Raynald eventually became the king of Belgium, but his brother Edward was very jealous. Edward convinced a group to follow him, and they overthrew Raynald's kingship. But Edward had compassion for Raynald and did not put him to death. Instead, he designed a special dungeon for him. It was a large circular room with one regular-sized doorway. It was outfitted with a bed, a table, and a chair. Edward included all the essentials Raynald would need to be fairly comfortable.

When the dungeon was completely built *around* Raynald, Edward paid him a visit. Edward pointed to the regular-sized doorway and called Raynald's attention to the fact there was no door in the opening. A door wasn't necessary to keep Raynald in the dungeon because he was grossly overweight—too fat to squeeze through the opening. Edward said to Raynald, "When you can fit through the doorway, you can leave."

King Edward then instructed his servants to bring massive platters of meat and other delicacies and daily place them on the table in Raynald's round dungeon room. The servants also filled the table with various kinds of pies and pastries. Many people accused Edward of being cruel, but he would respond, "My brother is not a prisoner. He can leave when he chooses to."

Now for the rest of the story: "Raynald remained in that same room, a prisoner of his own appetite, for more than ten years. He wasn't released until after Edward died in battle. By then Raynald's health was so far gone that he died within a year—not because he had no choice but because he would not use his power to choose what was best for his life."

This story graphically illustrates that even though people know what is wrong in their lives, it doesn't mean they will change. Sheer knowledge is not enough. The story also illustrates that people can feel very bad about their circumstances and still not change. Feeling bad is not enough. People must *choose* to change.

We have a choice. We can choose to have a positive attitude about resolving problems or we can continue with a negative spirit over issues of concern. We need to let go of the past and cease to blame people and circumstances. Taking responsibility for our lives is the road to mental health and inward peace.

Have you been locked in the dungeon of conflict with hurt and emotional pain? Would you like to experience freedom? Then you must do something. Walk through the doorway of communication, forgiveness, and reconciliation. There is no door. There is no lock. The choice is yours. *Now, that's an awesome thought, isn't it?*

The Spiritual Side of Conflict

Several years ago I attended a meeting where the speaker handed out paper and asked us to tear it into six equal pieces. He then asked us to write down on each piece of paper the six most important things in life to us—one item on each piece of paper. He mentioned that we might consider things like our health, our spouse, our children, our career, our friendships, our pets, and a number of other items. He then asked us to pick up those pieces of paper and hold them in one hand. He told us to fan them out so we could see them (like holding six playing cards).

Next, he talked about how conflict and tragedy come into the life of everyone. He mentioned that we can lose our job, we can lose our health, and we can lose our loved ones through death. Everything was going fine until he said, "We are going to imagine that tragedy is going to strike your life today. You will have to give up one of the six things in your hand—never to have it ever again. Pull out one of the pieces of paper and place it on the table in front of you."

Everyone groaned at the decision they had to make, but we followed the instructions.

The speaker talked a little more about tragedy, and told us that tragedy had just struck a second time. We would have to place another one of the six most important things in our lives on the table. More groans and rumblings could be heard throughout the audience as we gave up a second item—never to have it again.

This exercise in priorities continued until we only had one piece of paper in our hands. He said, "I want you to look at the piece of paper left in your hand. If you have anything written on it like an item of value or a person that you love, I want you to be aware that tragedy could strike and take that important thing from you. Then where would you be? If, however, you have written something like God or a relationship with God—that can never be taken from you." That turned out to be a very sobering evaluation of what was truly important to us.

#6

My Relationship
with God

I'm asking you the same question. If you went through the same exercise, what would be the most important thing in your life? Would it be things that could perish? Would it be a relationship with a loved one that could be lost? Or would you write down "my relationship with God"?

When it comes to spiritual matters, there seems to be three general categories of people. What category do you most identify with?

- *The "Whatevers."* These are people who couldn't care less about spiritual matters. They don't have any background in religious faith and don't feel a need to develop one. Or if they do have some previous knowledge, they have chosen to reject it for various reasons.

- *The "Ah-ahs!"* These are people who may or may not have some spiritual background but are interested in the topic. They are seekers who are open to consider this avenue of life and would like further information.

- *The "Thinkers."* These people are deeply concerned about spiritual matters. Their emotional and mental health is tied closely to their faith and how it affects their daily lives. They strive, in various degrees, to grow in their faith and knowledge.

People who are interested or are deeply concerned about spiritual matters identify with the words of Jesus when He said, "What will it profit a man if he gains the whole world and forfeits his soul? Or what will a man give in exchange for his soul?" (Matthew 16:26 NASB).

Jesus is simply saying that there is more to life than just material goods. He suggests that it's dangerous to not consider the deeper purposes of life. Have you ever wondered what life is all about? Have you questioned why there is pain and suffering...why people struggle with anxiety and depression...why there is so much conflict in the world? Have you ever wondered if God has a plan for your life?

You see, life is not always an easy road. Sometimes we encounter potholes of difficulties, bypasses of anxiety, pains of bumps, and detours of depression. During these times of uncomfortableness, it's easy to become weary of everything. Are you tired and weary of the pressures in your life and the various troubles you face? Then join the club. Many people feel the same way.

The Bible says God cares about you and the problems you face. God wants to come to your aid and help you through the tough times—the times that cause you anxiety and depression. He wants to help you in the conflicts you're facing. He wants to assist you in forgiving, reconciling, and restoring damaged relationships. Jesus said:

> Come to Me, all who are weary and heavy-laden, and I will give you rest. Take My yoke upon you and learn from Me, for I am gentle and humble in heart, and you will find rest for your souls. For My yoke is easy and My burden is light" (Matthew 11:28-30 NASB).

How does one come to Jesus? How does a person find rest for his or her soul? How can you experience peace in the midst of turmoil and conflict? Jesus said, "Peace I leave with you; My peace I give to you; not as the world gives do I give to you. Do not let your heart be troubled, nor let it be fearful" (John 14:27 NASB).

To experience peace *with* God and the peace *of* God, start with understanding who Jesus is. He is God in a human body. He came to tell you how to have a relationship with Him that will last for eternity.

When I was in Mongolia, a professor of literature, who was also a Parliament member, said to me: "I don't understand your God. He has three faces—Father, Son, and Holy Spirit. How can that be?" Here's part of the conversation that followed:

> "You're a professor of literature, are you not?" I said.
>
> "Yes, I am."
>
> "Is the name 'Shakespeare' familiar to you?"
>
> "Of course," he replied.
>
> "Are you acquainted with the character Macbeth?"
>
> "Yes, I am."
>
> "May I ask you a question? Could the character Macbeth ever meet the author Shakespeare?"
>
> He thought for a moment and replied, "'No, he could not."
>
> "Ah, but he could," I said. "All the author would have to do is write himself into the play and then introduce himself to Macbeth. That's what God the Father did when He wrote Himself into the play of life in the form of the Son Jesus of Nazareth. He became the God-Man."

God is a perfect and holy being. We humans aren't perfect. We aren't holy. We have imperfections. Try as we might, we often fall short of doing the right thing, saying the right thing, or thinking the right thing. Do you know anyone who is perfect?

This imperfection, or sin, is what separates us from a holy God. So God has a problem. He loves us, but He must also deal with our sinfulness—our imperfections. His Son was sent to die in our place...to pay our penalty for our sins...and to buy us back from the slave market of sinfulness and wickedness.

Jesus bore our sins on the cross. He died in our place. He was buried for our cruelty. And He rose from the grave to establish a new life and relationship with God for us. All we have to do is to have faith in this event.

The apostle Paul stated it this way:

> If you confess with your mouth Jesus as Lord, and believe in your heart that God raised Him from the dead, you will be saved; for with the heart a person believes, resulting in righteousness, and with the mouth he confesses, resulting in salvation...For "Whoever will call on the name of the Lord will be saved" (Romans 10:9-10,13 NASB).

Have you ever done that? If not, you can do it right now. Just put down this book and pray a simple prayer of faith asking Jesus to come into your life. Thank Him for dying in your place. Thank Him for providing a new relationship with God. Ask God to bring people into your life who will help you grow spiritually and learn more about God, Jesus, the Holy Spirit, and the Bible. Thank Jesus for saving you.

Do you remember flying a kite when you were a child? You would run with the kite held high until the wind caught it, and it began to soar into the sky. If you had a long string, the kite would rise higher and higher. Eventually, the kite would be so high that it would seem to disappear. The way you could tell the kite was still there was by the tug on the string caused by the wind blowing the kite. In the same way, God gives a tug on the strings of your heart. Something inside of you will sense God calling you to make a decision for Christ. Right now you may feel like I'm talking to you personally. If you have that feeling, it's the tug of God. It's certainly not my writing that's stirring your soul. I'm only a messenger bringing you the "good news" of Jesus Christ.

You may or may not be a person of faith. Regardless, the principles presented in this book will be effective if you put them into practice. The advantage of being a person of faith is that when the going gets rough and you feel like giving up, God will come to your aid if you ask Him to. He will give you the strength to do more than you think you can.

When someone invites Jesus to come into his or her life, God sends

His Holy Spirit to dwell within them. The Holy Spirit teaches you about God and supports you in tough times. He helps you endure pain and suffering that's been ravaging you because of anxiety, depression, and conflict . He will teach you how to overcome negative feelings, and He will help you pray when you don't know what to say.

To encourage you in the decision you just made to accept Jesus, I suggest you look up these verses in the Bible and write them out to help you remember them:

- Revelation 3:20:

- Colossians 1:14,27:

- 1 John 5:11-13:

- John 6:37:

- Romans 10:9-13:

- Hebrews 13:5:

What do these verses teach you?

Simple Bible-Reading Plan

Read the Bible every day. Here is a simple, daily Bible-study plan.

A. Select one of the books within the Bible you would like to read. A good book to start with would be the fourth book in the New Testament—the Gospel of John.

B. Read one chapter a day until you are finished with that book.

C. As you read each chapter, make some notes. Identify the following:

    1. The key verse of the chapter. [Central thought]

    2. God's commands. [A command is something to do]

    3. God's promises. [A promise is something to be believed]

    4. A short summary of the chapter.

5. Personal applications that you received from reading that particular chapter which you can apply to your daily life.

D. Look up 1 Peter 2:2 and Psalm 119:9,11. Talk to God daily in prayer, and keep your relationship with Him growing. Read 1 John 1:9; Psalm 66:18; and Philippians 4:6-7.

Fellowship with other believers. Get involved in a local church where the truth about Jesus is taught. Read Hebrews 10:23-25.

Tell others about Jesus. Discover where you can serve God. Help others grow in their faith. Look up Matthew 28:19-20; Mark 5:19; Acts 1:8; Ephesians 4:29; and 1 Corinthians 10:31. What did you learn from reading these Bible verses?

GOLD IN THE FIRE

He sat by a fire of seven-fold heat,
As He watched by the precious ore,
And closer He bent with a searching gaze
As He heated it more and more.
He knew He had ore that could stand the test,
And He wanted the finest gold
To mould as a crown for the King to wear,
Set with gems with a price untold.
So He laid our gold in the burning fire,
Tho' we fain would have said to Him, "Nay,"
And He watched the dross that we had not seen,
And it melted and passed away.
And the gold grew brighter and yet more bright,
But our eyes were so dim with tears,
We saw but the fire—not the Master's hand,
And questioned with anxious fears.
Yet our gold shone out with a richer glow,
As it mirrored a Form above,

That bent o'er the fire, tho' unseen by us,
With a look of ineffable love.
Can we think that it pleases His loving heart
To cause us a moment's pain?
Ah, no! But He saw through the present cross
The bliss of eternal gain.
So He waited there with a watchful eye,
With a love that is strong and sure,
And His gold did not suffer a bit more heat,
Than was needed to make it pure.*

AUTHOR UNKNOWN

I encourage you to begin today with some of the principles you've learned in this book. Begin the new patterns of behavior that will create more cohesiveness in your personal and professional relationships. Allow yourself the normal, temporary setbacks as you grow in your new habits. As you press forward, never give up. I pray that your life will become more rewarding and enriching as every day passes.

To give you more encouragement and wisdom, the next section of this book provides passages from the Bible that address conflict. As you reflect on them, I hope you will be inspired to put God's wisdom into practice. I'm reminded of these words from Charles Swindoll:

If finding God's way in the suddenness of storms makes our faith grow broad—then trusting God's wisdom in the "dailyness" of living makes it grow deep. And strong. Whatever may be your circumstances—however long it may have lasted—wherever you may be today, I bring you this reminder: The stronger the winds, the deeper the roots, and the longer the winds...the more beautiful the tree.

---

* Quoted in L.B.E. Cowman, *Streams in the Desert*

POINT TO PONDER

Can you imagine letting go of this conflict and releasing it forever? If you did, what kind of person would you become? What would it take for you to do so?

KENNETH CLOKE

Biblical Wisdom for
Reducing Relationship Conflicts

Note: Scripture verses in this section are quoted
from the New International Version.

Forgiveness

Proverbs 19:11: "A person's wisdom yields patience; it is to one's glory to overlook an offense."

Proverbs 24:17: "Do not gloat when your enemy falls; when they stumble, do not let your heart rejoice."

Proverbs 24:29: "Do not say, 'I'll do to them as they have done to me; I'll pay them back for what they did.'"

Proverbs 25:21-22: "If your enemy is hungry, give him food to eat; if he is thirsty, give him water to drink. In doing this, you will heap burning coals on his head, and the Lord will reward you."

Ecclesiastes 7:21-22: "Do not pay attention to every word people say, or you may hear your servant cursing you—for you know in your heart that many times you yourself have cursed others."

Matthew 5:7: "Blessed are the merciful, for they will be shown mercy."

Matthew 5:39-42: "I tell you, do not resist an evil person. If someone slaps you on the right cheek, turn to them the other cheek also. And if anyone wants to sue you and take your shirt, hand over your coat as well. If anyone forces you to go one mile, go with them two miles."

Matthew 5:43-48: "You have heard that it was said, 'Love your neighbor and hate your enemy.' But I tell you, love your enemies and pray for those who persecute you, that you may be children of your Father in heaven. He causes his sun to rise on the evil and the good, and sends rain on the righteous and the unrighteous. If you love those who love you, what reward will you get? Are not even the tax collectors doing that? And if you greet only your own people, what are you doing more than others? Do not even pagans do that? Be perfect, therefore, as your heavenly Father is perfect."

Matthew 6:12: "Forgive us our debts, as we also have forgiven our debtors."

Matthew 6:14-15: "If you forgive other people when they sin against you, your heavenly Father will also forgive you. But if you do not forgive others their sins, your Father will not forgive your sins."

Matthew 18:21-22: "Peter came to Jesus and asked, 'Lord, how many times shall I forgive my brother or sister who sins against me? Up to seven times?' Jesus answered, 'I tell you, not seven times, but seventy-seven times.'"

Mark 11:25: "When you stand praying, if you hold anything against anyone, forgive them, so that your Father in heaven may forgive you your sins."

Luke 6:27-37: "Love your enemies, do good to those who hate you, bless those who curse you, pray for those who mistreat you. If someone slaps you on one cheek, turn to them the other also. If someone takes your coat, do not withhold your shirt from them. Give to everyone who asks you, and if anyone takes what belongs to you, do not demand it back. Do to others as you would have them do to you.

"If you love those who love you, what credit is that to you? Even sinners love those who love them. And if you do good to those who are good to you, what credit is that to you? Even sinners do that. And if you lend to those from whom you expect repayment, what credit is that to you? Even sinners lend to sinners, expecting to be repaid in full. But love your enemies, do good to them, and lend to them without expecting to get anything back. Then your reward will be great, and you will be children of the Most High, because he is kind to the ungrateful and wicked. Be merciful, just as your Father is merciful. Do not judge, and you will not be judged. Do not condemn, and you will not be condemned. Forgive, and you will be forgiven."

Luke 11:4: "Forgive us our sins, for we also forgive everyone who sins against us."

Luke 17:3-4: "If your brother or sister sins against you, rebuke them; and if they repent, forgive them. Even if they sin against you seven times in a day and seven times come back to you saying 'I repent,' you must forgive them."

Romans 12:14-16: "Bless those who persecute you; bless and do not curse. Rejoice with those who rejoice; mourn with those who mourn. Live in harmony with one another."

Romans 12:17-21: "Do not repay anyone evil for evil. Be careful to do what is right in the eyes of everyone. If it is possible, as far as it depends on you, live at peace with everyone. Do not take revenge, my dear friends, but leave room for God's wrath, for it is written: 'It is mine to avenge; I will repay,' says the Lord. On the contrary: 'If your enemy is hungry, feed him; if he is thirsty, give him something to drink. In doing this, you will heap burning coals on his head.' Do not be overcome by evil, but overcome evil with good."

1 Corinthians 4:12-13: "We work hard with our own hands. When we are cursed, we bless; when we are persecuted, we endure it; when we are slandered, we answer kindly."

Ephesians 4:32: "Be kind and compassionate to one another, forgiving each other, just as in Christ God forgave you."

Colossians 3:13-14: "Bear with each other and forgive one another whatever if any of you has a grievance against someone. Forgive as the Lord forgave you. And over all these virtues put on love, which binds them all together in perfect unity."

1 Peter 3:9-11: "Do not repay evil with evil or insult with insult. On the contrary, repay evil with blessing, because to this you were called so that you may inherit a blessing. For, 'Whoever would love life and see good days must keep their tongue from evil and their lips from deceitful speech. They must turn from evil and do good; they must seek peace and pursue it.'"

Love

Proverbs 10:12: "Hatred stirs up conflict, but love covers over all wrongs."

Proverbs 15:17: "Better a small serving of vegetables with love than a fattened calf with hatred."

Proverbs 17:9: "Whoever would foster love covers over an offense, but whoever repeats the matter separates close friends."

John 13:34-35: "A new command I give you: Love one another. As I have loved you, so you must love one another. By this everyone will know that you are my disciples, if you love one another."

John 15:12-14: Jesus said, "My command is this: Love each other as I have loved you. Greater love has no one than this: to lay down one's life for one's friends. You are my friends if you do what I command."

John 15:17: Jesus said, "This is my command: Love each other."

Romans 13:8: "Let no debt remain outstanding, except the continuing debt to love one another, for whoever loves others has fulfilled the law."

1 Corinthians 13:13: "Now these three remain: faith, hope and love. But the greatest of these is love."

1 Corinthians 16:14: "Do everything in love."

Galatians 5:13-15: "You, my brothers and sisters, were called to be free. But do not use your freedom to indulge the flesh; rather, serve one another humbly in love. For the entire law is fulfilled in keeping this one command: 'Love your neighbor as yourself.' If you bite and devour each other, watch out or you will be destroyed by each other."

Galatians 5:22-23: "The fruit of the Spirit is love, joy, peace, forbearance, kindness, goodness, faithfulness, gentleness and self-control."

Philippians 2:2-4: "Make my joy complete by being like-minded, having the same love, being one in spirit and of one mind. Do nothing out of selfish ambition or vain conceit. Rather, in humility value others above yourselves, not looking to your own interests but each of you to the interests of others."

Colossians 3:13-14: "Bear with each other and forgive one another if any of you has a grievance against someone. Forgive as the Lord forgave you. And over all these virtues put on love, which binds them all together in perfect unity."

1 Thessalonians 4:9: "Now about your love for one another we do not need to write to you, for you yourselves have been taught by God to love each other."

Hebrews 10:24: "Let us consider how we may spur one another on toward love and good deeds."

1 Peter 1:22: "Now that you have purified yourselves by obeying the truth so that you have sincere love for each other, love one another deeply, from the heart."

1 Peter 4:8: "Above all, love each other deeply, because love covers over a multitude of sins."

1 John 2:9-11: "Anyone who claims to be in the light but hates a brother or sister is still in the darkness. Anyone who loves their brother and sister lives in the light, and there is nothing in them to make them stumble. But anyone who hates a brother or sister is in the darkness and walks around in the darkness. They do not know where they are going, because the darkness has blinded them."

1 John 3:11-12: "This is the message you heard from the beginning: We should love one another."

1 John 3:14-15: "We know that we have passed from death to life, because we love each other. Anyone who does not love remains in death. Anyone who hates a brother or sister is a murderer, and you know that no murderer has eternal life residing in him."

1 John 4:11-12: "Dear friends, since God so loved us, we also ought to love one another. No one has ever seen God; but if we love one another, God lives in us and his love is made complete in us."

1 John 4:19-21: "Whoever claims to love God yet hates a brother or sister is a liar. For whoever does not love their brother and sister, whom they have seen, cannot love God, whom they have not seen. And he has given us this command: Anyone who loves God must also love their brother and sister."

2 John 5-6: "And now, dear lady, I am not writing you a new command but one we have had from the beginning. I ask that we love one another. And this is love: that we walk in obedience to his commands. As you have heard from the beginning, his command is that you walk in love."

Patience

Psalm 37:7: "Be still before the LORD and wait patiently for him; do not fret when people succeed in their ways, when they carry out their wicked schemes."

Proverbs 15:18: "A hot-tempered person stirs up conflict, but the one who is patient calms a quarrel."

Ecclesiastes 7:8: "The end of a matter is better than its beginning, and patience is better than pride."

Romans 5:3-5: "We also glory in our sufferings, because we know that suffering produces perseverance; perseverance, character; and character, hope. And hope does not put us to shame, because God's love has been poured out into our hearts through the Holy Spirit, who has been given to us."

1 Corinthians 13:4-7: "Love is patient, love is kind. It does not envy, it does not boast, it is not proud. It does not dishonor others, it is not self-seeking, it is not easily angered, it keeps no record of wrongs. Love does not delight in evil but rejoices with the truth. It always protects, always trusts, always hopes, always perseveres."

Galatians 6:9-10: "Let us not become weary in doing good, for at the proper time we will reap a harvest if we do not give up. Therefore, as we have opportunity, let us do good to all people, especially to those who belong to the family of believers."

Ephesians 4:1-3: "As a prisoner for the Lord, then, I urge you to live a life worthy of the calling you have received. Be completely humble and gentle; be patient, bearing with one another in love. Make every effort to keep the unity of the Spirit through the bond of peace."

Colossians 3:12-14: "As God's chosen people, holy and dearly loved, clothe yourselves with compassion, kindness, humility, gentleness and patience. Bear with each other and forgive one another if any of you has a grievance against someone. Forgive as the Lord forgave you. And over all these virtues put on love, which binds them all together in perfect unity."

1 Thessalonians 5:14-15: "We urge you, brothers and sisters, warn those who are idle and disruptive, encourage the disheartened, help the weak, be patient with everyone. Make sure that nobody pays back wrong for wrong, but always strive to do what is good for each other and for everyone else."

2 Timothy 2:24-26: "The Lord's servant must not be quarrelsome but must be kind to everyone, able to teach, not resentful. Opponents must be gently instructed, in the hope that God will grant them repentance leading them to a knowledge of the truth, and that they will come to their senses and escape from the trap of the devil, who has taken them captive to do his will."

James 1:19-20: "My dear brothers and sisters, take note of this: Everyone should be quick to listen, slow to speak and slow to become angry, because human anger does not produce the righteousness that God desires."

1 Peter 2:19-24: "It is commendable if someone bears up under the pain of unjust suffering because they are conscious of God. But how is it to your credit if you receive a beating for doing wrong and endure it? But if you suffer for doing good and you endure it, this is commendable before God. To this you were called, because Christ suffered for you, leaving you an example, that you should follow in his steps. 'He committed no sin, and no deceit was found in his mouth.' When they hurled their insults at him, he did not retaliate; when he suffered, he made no threats. Instead, he entrusted himself to him who judges justly."

Peace

Psalm 34:14: "Turn from evil and do good; seek peace and pursue it."

Psalm 133:1: "How good and pleasant it is when God's people live together in unity!"

Proverbs 12:20: "Deceit is in the hearts of those who plot evil, but those who promote peace have joy."

Proverbs 15:17: "Better a small serving of vegetables with love than a fattened calf with hatred."

Proverbs 16:7: "When the LORD takes pleasure in anyone's way, he causes their enemies to make peace with them."

Proverbs 17:1: "Better a dry crust with peace and quiet than a house full of feasting, with strife."

Proverbs 17:14: "Starting a quarrel is like breaching a dam; so drop the matter before a dispute breaks out."

Proverbs 20:3: "It is to one's honor to avoid strife, but every fool is quick to quarrel."

Matthew 5:9: "Blessed are the peacemakers, for they will be called children of God."

Mark 9:50: "Salt is good, but if it loses its saltiness, how can you make it salty again? Have salt among yourselves, and be at peace with each other."

Romans 14:19: "Let us therefore make every effort to do what leads to peace and to mutual edification."

1 Corinthians 14:33: "God is not a God of disorder but of peace."

Ephesians 4:3: "Make every effort to keep the unity of the Spirit through the bond of peace."

1 Thessalonians 5:13: "Live in peace with each other."

Hebrews 12:14: "Make every effort to live in peace with everyone and to be holy; without holiness no one will see the Lord."

James 3:17-18: "The wisdom that comes from heaven is first of all pure; then peace-loving, considerate, submissive, full of mercy and good fruit, impartial and sincere. Peacemakers who sow in peace reap a harvest of righteousness."

Revenge

Leviticus 19:18: "Do not seek revenge or bear a grudge against anyone among your people, but love your neighbor as yourself. I am the LORD."

Proverbs 20:22: "Do not say, 'I'll pay you back for this wrong!' Wait for the LORD, and he will avenge you."

Proverbs 24:29: "Do not say, 'I'll do to them as they have done to me; I'll pay them back for what they did.'"

Proverbs 26:27: "Whoever digs a pit will fall into it; if someone rolls a stone, it will roll back on them."

Matthew 7:1-2: "Do not judge, or you too will be judged. For in the same way you judge others, you will be judged, and with the measure you use, it will be measured to you."

Romans 12:19: "Do not take revenge, my dear friends, but leave room for God's wrath, for it is written: 'It is mine to avenge; I will repay,' says the Lord."

1 Thessalonians 5:14-15: "Make sure that nobody pays back wrong for wrong, but always strive to do what is good for each other and for everyone else."

1 Peter 3:9-12: "Do not repay evil with evil or insult with insult. On the contrary, repay evil with blessing, because to this you were called so that you may inherit a blessing. For, 'whoever would love life and see good days must keep their tongue from evil and their lips from deceitful speech. They must turn from evil and do good; they must seek peace and pursue it. For the eyes of the Lord are on the righteous and his ears are attentive to their prayer, but the face of the Lord is against those who do evil.'"

Biblical Wisdom on the Power of Words and Behavior

Note: Scriptures in this section are quoted from the Living Bible.

1 Samuel 15:16-23: "Samuel said to Saul, 'Stop! Listen to what the Lord told me last night!'

"'What was it?' Saul asked.

"And Samuel told him, 'When you didn't think much of yourself, God made you king of Israel. And he sent you on an errand and told you, "Go and completely destroy the sinners, the Amalekites, until they are all dead."' [Question to Saul] 'Then why didn't you obey the Lord? Why did you rush for the loot and do exactly what God said not to?'

[Saul's rationalization, justification, excuses] "'But I have obeyed the Lord,' Saul insisted. 'I did what he told me to; and I brought King Agag but killed everyone else. And it was only when my troops demanded it that I let them keep the best of the sheep and oxen and loot to sacrifice to the Lord.'

"Samuel replied [stating the problem], 'Has the Lord as much pleasure in your burnt offerings and sacrifices as in your obedience?' [the responsibility] 'Obedience is far better than sacrifice. He is much more interested in your listening to him than in your offering the fat of rams to him.' [What disobedience and rebellion equals] 'For rebellion is as bad as the sin of witchcraft, and stubbornness is as bad as worshiping idols.' [The result] 'And now because you have rejected the word of Jehovah, he has rejected you from being king.'"

Proverbs 6:16: "There are six things the Lord hates—no, seven: haughtiness, lying, murdering, plotting evil, eagerness to do wrong, a false witness, sowing discord among brothers."

Proverbs 10:14: "A wise man holds his tongue. Only a fool blurts out everything he knows; that only leads to sorrow and trouble."

Proverbs 10:19-21: "Don't talk so much. You keep putting your foot in your mouth. Be sensible and turn off the flow! When a good man speaks, he is worth listening to, but the words of fools are a dime a dozen. A godly man gives good advice, but a rebel is destroyed by lack of common sense."

Proverbs 11:12-13: "To quarrel with a neighbor is foolish; a man with good sense holds his tongue. A gossip goes around spreading rumors, while a trustworthy man tries to quiet them."

Proverbs 12:18: "Some people like to make cutting remarks, but the words of the wise soothe and heal."

Proverbs 12:23: "A wise man doesn't display his knowledge, but a fool displays his foolishness."

Proverbs 13:2-3: "The good man wins his case by careful argument; the evil-minded only wants to fight. Self-control means controlling the tongue! A quick retort can ruin everything."

Proverbs 15:1: "A gentle answer turns away wrath, but harsh words cause quarrels."

Proverbs 15:4-5: "Gentle words cause life and health; griping brings discouragement. Only a fool despises his father's advice; a wise son considers each suggestion."

Proverbs 15:28: "A good man thinks before he speaks; the evil man pours out his evil words without a thought."

Proverbs 17:19: "Sinners love to fight; boasting is looking for trouble."

Proverbs 18:6-8: "A fool gets into constant fights. His mouth is his undoing! His words endanger him. What dainty morsels rumors are. They are eaten with great relish!"

Proverbs 18:19: "It is harder to win back the friendship of an offended brother than to capture a fortified city. His anger shuts you out like iron bars."

Proverbs 19:11: "A wise man restrains his anger and overlooks insults. This is to his credit."

Proverbs 20:3: "It is an honor for a man to stay out of a fight. Only fools insist on quarreling."

Proverbs 21:23: "Keep your mouth closed and you'll stay out of trouble."

Proverbs 22:10: "Throw out the mocker, and you will be rid of tension, fighting, and quarrels."

Proverbs 25:18: "Telling lies about someone is as harmful as hitting him with an ax, or wounding him with a sword, or shooting him with a sharp arrow."

Proverbs 26:21-23: "A quarrelsome man starts fights as easily as a match sets fire to paper. Gossip is a dainty morsel eaten with great relish. Pretty words may hide a wicked heart, just as a pretty glaze covers a common clay pot."

Proverbs 29:8-9: "Fools start fights everywhere while wise men try to keep peace. There's no use arguing with a fool. He only rages and scoffs, and tempers flare."

Matthew 12:34-37: "A man's heart determines his speech. A good man's speech reveals the rich treasures within him. An evil-hearted man is filled with venom, and his speech reveals it. And I tell you this, that you must give account on Judgment Day for every idle word you speak. Your words now reflect your fate then: either you will be justified by them or you will be condemned."

Matthew 15:16-20: " 'Don't you understand?' Jesus asked him. 'Don't you see that anything you eat passes through the digestive tract and out again? But evil words come from an evil heart and defile the man who says them. For from the heart come evil thoughts, murder, adultery, fornication, theft, lying, and slander. These are what defile; but there is no spiritual defilement from eating without first going through the ritual of ceremonial hand washing!' "

Ephesians 4:31-32: "Stop being mean, bad-tempered, and angry. Quarreling, harsh words, and dislike of others should have no place in your lives. Instead, be kind to each other, tenderhearted, forgiving one another, just as God has forgiven you because you belong to Christ."

Ephesians 5:19-20: "Talk with each other much about the Lord, quoting psalms and hymns and singing sacred songs, making music in your hearts to the Lord. Always give thanks for everything to our God and Father in the name of our Lord Jesus Christ."

2 Timothy 2:14-17: "Remind your people of these great facts, and command them in the name of the Lord not to argue over unimportant things. Such arguments are confusing and useless and even harmful. Work hard so God can say to you, 'Well done.' Be a good workman, one who does not need to be ashamed when God examines your work. Know what his Word says and means. Steer clear of foolish discussions that lead people into the sin of anger with each other. Things will be said that will burn and hurt for a long time to come."

James 1:26-2:1: "Anyone who says he is a Christian but doesn't control his sharp tongue is just fooling himself, and his religion isn't worth much. The Christian who is pure and without fault, from God the Father's point of view, is the one who takes care of orphans and widows, and who remains true to the Lord—not soiled and dirtied by his contacts with the world."

James 3:1-18: "Dear brothers, don't be too eager to tell others their faults, for we all make many mistakes; and when we teachers of religion, who should know better, do wrong, our punishment will be greater than it would be for others.

"If anyone can control his tongue, it proves that he has perfect control over himself in every other way. We can make a large horse turn around and go wherever we want by means of a small bit in his mouth. And a tiny rudder makes a huge ship turn wherever the pilot wants it to go, even though the winds are strong. So also the tongue is a small thing, but what enormous damage it can do. A great forest can be set on fire by one tiny spark. And the tongue is a flame of fire. It is full of wickedness, and poisons every part of the body. And the tongue is set on fire by hell itself and can turn our whole lives into a blazing flame of destruction and disaster.

"Men have trained, or can train, every kind of animal or bird that lives and every kind of reptile and fish, but no human being can tame the tongue. It is always ready to pour out its deadly poison. Sometimes it praises our heavenly Father, and sometimes it breaks out into curses against men who are made like God. And so blessing and cursing come pouring out of the same mouth. Dear brothers, surely this is not right! Does a spring of water bubble out first with fresh water and then with bitter water? Can you pick olives from a fig tree, or figs from a grape vine? No, and you can't draw fresh water from a salty pool.

"If you are wise, live a life of steady goodness so that only good deeds will pour forth. And if you don't brag about them, then you will be truly wise! And by all means don't brag about being wise and good if you are bitter and jealous and selfish; that is the worst sort of lie. For jealousy and selfishness are not God's kind of wisdom. Such things are earthly, unspiritual, inspired by the devil. For wherever there is jealousy or selfish ambition, there will be disorder and every other kind of evil.

"But the wisdom that comes from heaven is first of all pure and full of quiet gentleness. Then it is peace-loving and courteous. It allows discussion and is willing to yield to others; it is full of mercy and good deeds. It is wholehearted and straightforward and sincere. And those who are peacemakers will plant seeds of peace and reap a harvest of goodness."

James 4:1-3: "What is causing the quarrels and fights among you? Isn't it because there is a whole army of evil desires within you? You want what you don't have, so you kill to get it. You long for what others have, and can't afford it, so you start a fight to take it away from them. And yet the reason you don't have what you want is that you don't ask God for it. And even when you do ask you don't get it because your whole aim is wrong—you want only what will give you pleasure."

1 Peter 2:13-25: "For the Lord's sake, obey every law of your government: those of the king as head of the state, and those of the king's officers, for he has sent them to punish all who do wrong, and to honor those who do right.

"It is God's will that your good lives should silence those who foolishly condemn the Gospel without knowing what it can do for them, having never experienced its power. You are free from the law, but that doesn't mean you are free to do wrong. Live as those who are free to do only God's will at all times. Show respect for everyone. Love Christians everywhere. Fear God and honor the government.

"Servants, you must respect your masters and do whatever they tell you—not only if they are kind and reasonable, but even if they are tough and cruel. Praise the Lord if you are punished for doing right! Of course, you get no credit for being patient if you are beaten for doing wrong; but if you do right and suffer for it, and are patient beneath the blows, God is well pleased.

"This suffering is all part of the work God has given you. Christ, who suffered for you, is your example. Follow in his steps: He never sinned, never told a lie, never answered back when insulted; when he suffered he did not threaten to get even; he left his case in the hands of God who always judges fairly. He personally carried the load of our sins in his own body when he died on the cross so that we can be finished with sin and live a good life from now on. For his wounds have healed ours! Like sheep you wandered away from God, but now you have returned to your Shepherd, the Guardian of your souls who keeps you safe from all attacks."

1 Peter 3:8-18: "You should be like one big happy family, full of sympathy toward each other, loving one another with tender hearts and humble minds. Don't repay evil for evil. Don't snap back at those who say unkind things about you. Instead, pray for God's help for them, for we are to be kind to others, and God will bless us for it.

"If you want a happy, good life, keep control of your tongue, and guard your lips from telling lies. Turn away from evil and do good. Try to live in peace even if you must run after it to catch and hold it! For the Lord is watching his children, listening to their prayers; but the Lord's face is hard against those who do evil.

"Usually no one will hurt you for wanting to do good. But even if they should, you are to be envied, for God will reward you for it. Quietly trust yourself to Christ your Lord, and if anybody asks why you believe as you do, be ready to tell him, and do it in a gentle and respectful way. Do what is right; then if men speak against you, calling you evil names, they will become ashamed of themselves for falsely accusing you when you have only done what is good. Remember, if God wants you to suffer, it is better to suffer for doing good than for doing wrong! Christ also suffered. He died once for the sins of all us guilty sinners although he himself was innocent of any sin at any time, that he might bring us safely home to God. But though his body died, his spirit lived on."

Philippians 2:1-16: "Is there any such thing as Christians cheering each other up? Do you love me enough to want to help me? Does it mean anything to you that we are brothers in the Lord, sharing the same Spirit? Are your hearts tender and sympathetic at all? Then make me truly happy by loving each other and agreeing wholeheartedly with each other, working together with one heart and mind and purpose.

"Don't be selfish; don't live to make a good impression on others. Be humble, thinking of others as better than yourself. Don't just think about your own affairs, but be interested in others, too, and in what they are doing.

"Your attitude should be the kind that was shown us by Jesus Christ, who, though he was God, did not demand and cling to his rights as God, but laid aside his mighty power and glory, taking the disguise of a slave and becoming like men. And he humbled himself even further, going so far as actually to die a criminal's death on a cross.

"Yet it was because of this that God raised him up to the heights of heaven and gave him a name which is above every other name, that at the name of Jesus every knee shall bow in heaven and on earth and under the earth, and every tongue shall confess that Jesus Christ is Lord, to the glory of God the Father.

"Dearest friends, when I was there with you, you were always so careful to follow my instructions. And now that I am away you must be even more careful to do the good things that result from being saved, obeying God with deep reverence, shrinking back from all that might displease him. For God is at work within you, helping you want to obey him, and then helping you do what he wants.

"In everything you do, stay away from complaining and arguing so that no one can speak a word of blame against you. You are to live clean, innocent lives as children of God in a dark world full of people who are crooked and stubborn. Shine out among them like beacon lights, holding out to them the Word of Life."

Bibliography

Adams, Jay E. *How to Help People Change*. Grand Rapids, MI: Zondervan Publishing Company, 1986.

Adler, Alfred. *Understanding Human Nature*. New York: Fawcett Premier Books, 1927.

Ahlem, Lloyd H. *How to Cope with Conflict and Change*. Glendale, CA: Regal Books, 1978.

Alyn, Kimberly, and Bob Phillips. *Men Are Slobs and Women Are Neat*. Eugene, OR: Harvest House Publishers, 2004.

Bolton, Robert. *People Skills*. New York: Simon and Schuster, 1979.

Cloke, Kenneth. *The Crossroads of Conflict*. Calgary, AB: Janis Publications, 2006.

Cloke, Kenneth. *Mediation: Revenge and the Magic of Forgiveness*. Santa Monica, CA: Center for Dispute Resolution, 1994.

Cloke, Kenneth, and Joan Goldsmith. *Resolving Conflicts at Work*. San Francisco: John Wiley and Sons, Inc., 2005.

Collins, Gary. *How to Be a People Helper*. Santa Ana, CA: Vision House Publishers, 1976.

Condon, John C. *Interpersonal Communication*. New York: Macmillan Publishing, 1977.

Cosgrove, Charles H., and Dennis D. Hatfield. *Church Conflict*. Nashville: Abington Press, 1994.

Costantino, Cathy A., and Christina Sickles Merchant. *Designing Conflict Management Systems*. San Francisco: Jossey-Bass, 1996.

Cowman, L.B.E. *Streams in the Desert* (Grand Rapids, MI: Zondervan, 1996). "Gold in the Fire," quoted for October 29, author unknown.

Dawson, Roger. *Secrets of Power Negotiating*. Franklin Lakes, NJ: Career Press, 2001.

Dues, Michael. *The Art of Conflict Management: Achieving Solutions for Life, Work, and Beyond*. Chantilly, VA: The Great Courses, 2010.

Ferguson, Ben. *God, I've Got a Problem*. Santa Ana, CA: Vision House, 1974.

Filley, Alan C. *Interpersonal Conflict Resolution*. Palo Alto, CA: Scott, Foresman and Company, 1975.

Fisher, Roger, and William Ury. *Getting to Yes*. New York: Penguin Books, 1981.

Flynn, Leslie B. *Great Church Fights*. Wheaton, IL: Victor Books, 1976.

Girdano, Daniel, and George Everly. *Controlling Stress and Tension*. Englewood Cliffs, NJ: Prentice-Hall, 1979.

Graham, Scott. *Resolving Conflict with Others and Within Yourself.* Oakland, CA: New Harbinger Publications, Inc., 1990.

Grant, Wendy. *Resolving Conflicts: How to Turn Conflict into Co-operation.* Rockport, MA: Element Books, Inc., 1997.

Haggai, John Edmund. *How to Win over Worry.* Grand Rapids, MI: Zondervan Publishing House, 1959.

Howe, Reuel L. *The Miracle of Dialogue.* New York: The Seabury Press, 1963.

Human Communication Research, vol. 9, no. 1, Transaction, Inc., copyright © 1982. All charts pp. 85-86. Used by permission.

Hunt, June. *How to Forgive...When You Don't Feel like It.* Eugene, OR: Harvest House Publishers, 2007.

Jandt, Fred E. *Conflict Resolution Through Communication.* New York: Harper and Row, Publishers, Inc., 1973.

Karrass, Chester L. *The Negotiating Game.* New York: Harper-Collins Publishers, 1992.

Kindler, Herbert S. *Managing Disagreement Constructively.* Menlo Park, CA: Crisp Publications, Inc., 1996.

Krebs, Richard L. *Creative Conflict.* Minneapolis: Augsburg Publishing House, 1982.

Kreider, Robert S., and Rachel Waltner Goossen. *When Good People Quarrel.* Scottsdale, PA: 1989.

LaHaye, Tim, and Bob Phillips. *Anger Is a Choice.* Grand Rapids, MI: Zondervan Publishing House, 1982.

Liberman, David J. *Never Be Lied to Again.* New York: St. Martin's Press, 1998.

Lum, Grande. *The Negotiation Fieldbook.* New York: McGraw Hill, 2011.

Lutzer, Erwin. *Managing Your Emotions.* Chappaqua, NY: Christian Herald Books, 1981.

Navarro, Joe. *What Every Body Is Saying.* New York: Harper-Collins Publishers, 2008.

Nierenberg, Gerard I. *The Art of Negotiating.* New York: Hawthorne Books, Inc., 1968.

Nierenberg, Gerard I.; and Henry H. Calero. *How to Read a Person like a Book.* New York: Pocket Book, 1973.

Noonan, William R. *Discussing the Undiscussable.* San Francisco: John Wiley and Sons, Inc., 2007.

Osborne, Christina. *Dealing with Difficult People.* New York: DK Publishing, 2002.

Patterson, Grenny, and Switzler McMillan. *Crucial Conversations.* New York: McGraw Hill, 2012.

Pease, Allan. *Signals: How to Use Body Language for Power, Success, and Love.* New York: Bantam Books, 1981.

Phillips, Bob. *42 Days to Feeling Great.* Eugene, OR: Harvest House Publishers, 2001.

Phillips, Bob. *What to Do Until the Psychiatrist Comes.* Eugene, OR: Harvest House Publishers, 1995.

Phillips, Bob, and Kimberly Alyn. *How to Deal with Annoying People.* Eugene, OR: Harvest House Publishers, 2003.

Pickering, Peg. *How to Manage Conflict.* Franklin Lakes, NJ: National Press Publications, 2000.

Poirier, Alfred. *The Peacemaking Pastor*. Grand Rapids, MI: Baker Books, 2006.

Polsky, Lawrence, and Antoine Gerschel. *Perfect Phrases for Conflict Resolution*. New York: McGraw Hill Publishers, 2011.

Ruesch, Jurgen. *Disturbed Communication*. New York: W.W. Norton and Company, Inc., 1972.

Sande, Kenneth. *The Peacemaker*. Grand Rapids, MI: Baker Books, 2004.

Sande, Kenneth, and Kevin Johnson. *Resolving Everyday Conflict*. Grand Rapids, MI: Baker Books, 2011.

Scott, Gini Graham. *Resolving Conflict*. Oakland, CA: New Harbinger Publications, Inc., 1990.

Shell, G. Richard. *Bargaining for Advantage*. New York: Penguin Group, 2006.

Stone, Douglas, Bruce Patton, and Sheila Heen. *Difficult Conversations*. New York: Penguin Books, 2000.

Tennant, Don. *Spy the Lie*. New York: St. Martin Press, 2013.

Van Pelt, Nancy L. *How to Talk So Your Mate Will Listen*. Grand Rapids, MI: 2000.

Viscott, David. *The Language of Feelings*. New York: Pocket Books, 1976.

Viscott, David. *The Viscott Method*. New York: Pocket Books, 1984.

Wahlroos, Sven. *Family Communication*. New York: Macmillian Publishing Co., Inc., 1974.

Wainwright, Gordon R. *Body Language*. London: Hodder Headline Plc, 1985.

Wakefield, Norman. *Listening*. Waco, TX: Word Books, 1981.

Walters, Richard. *How to Say Hard Things the Easy Way*. Irving, TX: Word Publishing, 1991. Information in ch. 9 used by permission.

Weems, Lovett H. *Take the Next Step: Leading Lasting Change in the Church*. Nashville: Abingdon Press, 2003.

Weinhold, Barry K., and Janae B. Weinhold. *How to Break Free of the Drama Triangle and Victim Consciousness*. CreateSpace Independent Publishing Platform, https://www.createspace.com/, 2014.

Wilmont, William W., and Janet L. Hocker. *Interpersonal Conflict*. Dubuque, IA: Wm. C. Brown Publishers, 1985.

Other Helpful Books by Bob Phillips

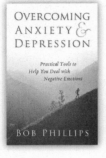

Overcoming Anxiety and Depression (Paperback and Ebook)

Anxiety and depression are the two most common emotions that plague people, causing emotional distress and feelings of inferiority, loneliness, and despair. Bob Phillips reveals the root causes of anxiety and depression, which are fear and anger, and he helps readers deal with these driving forces in an effective, godly way.

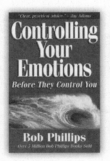

Controlling Your Emotions (Ebook and POD)

Bob provides practical help for cutting loose negative baggage and insights for dealing with depression, overcoming bitterness, and understanding feelings. True stories, emotional evaluations, personality charts, and biblical counsel make this book informative and easy-to-read.

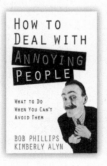

How to Deal with Annoying People (Ebook and POD)

Readers will discover why they are annoyed by others, why others are annoyed by them, and what they can do to create wholesome relationships. Churches, individuals, couples, employees, and managers can all learn to employ biblical principles along with a fun and simple process of identifying social cues.